Ann Anderson Evans is a writer, linguist, and professor. Twice a wife and once a widow, she's a mother and grandmother. She has traveled and lived in many countries and speaks six languages.

Her first book, *DARING TO DATE AGAIN* (SheWrites Press, 2014) won multiple prizes for memoir. Her story, *Precious Love* was nominated for a Pushcart Prize. Other short stories have been published in *Entropy, The Opiate, Pulse, Phantasmagoria, Forge, Under the Sun, Ozone Park Journal, Phoebe, The Raven's Perch, Words & Images, Pedagogy,* and *Better Than Starbucks.* Ann has appeared on television, radio, and podcasts, with appearances on The Discovery Channel's *Sex in America* special, NPR's *Author's Corner, The Author's Show, ArtistFirst, KGUA, Gualala, California, JenningsWire, Beyond Fifty Radio: Daniel Davis, Kim Power Stilson, Donna Seebo Show,* and *The Michael Dresser Show.*

She shares her experiences and insights using a well-traveled lifetime and a sense of humor and joy. She lives in Vermont.

Ann can be found at *www.annandersonevans.com.*

This book is for Terry and people like him.

Ann Anderson Evans

THE SWEET PAIN OF BEING ALIVE

A Memoir of Love and Death

AUSTIN MACAULEY PUBLISHERS™

LONDON * CAMBRIDGE * NEW YORK * SHARJAH

Ordering Information
Quantity sales: Special discounts are available on quantity purchases by corporations, associations, and others. For details, contact the publisher at the address below.

Publisher's Cataloging-in-Publication data
Evans, Ann Anderson
The Sweet Pain of Being Alive

ISBN 9798889104049 (Paperback)
ISBN 9798889104063 (ePub e-book)
ISBN 9798889104056 (Audiobook)

Library of Congress Control Number: 2023912530

www.austinmacauley.com/us

First Published 2024
Austin Macauley Publishers LLC
40 Wall Street, 33rd Floor, Suite 3302
New York, NY 10005
USA

mail-usa@austinmacauley.com
+1 (646) 5125767

Thanks to Lisa Dale Norton, who was a fine editor and sympathetic friend. Thanks also to Mark Malatesta, who showed me how this publishing thing worked and was always ready with an encouraging word.

Table of Contents

Foreword

In the last twenty years or so the number of people who describe themselves as transgender or gender non-binary has grown from a handful into millions. Western society and culture were ill-prepared to welcome, support and integrate these individuals into inclusive daily life. These people were, and in most cases are, treated as "other," and as such they are too often treated unkindly, even cruelly. All too rarely are they met with understanding and compassion.

As was the case with many of the societal changes that have been spawned by the internet and social media, changes in gender expression may have moved too fast for the average person to keep up. For most people, as well as most institutions, change is scary, and lack of understanding or awareness breeds fear and hostility. Even the most well-meaning and openhearted people can be clumsy and clueless when encountering a transgender person for the first time. And, it should be said, sometimes the expectations of transgender people who are "out" can be unrealistic in such situations.

During the 1960s and 70s there were a tiny handful of notorious cases of individuals who underwent gender reassignment surgery. Their cases were reported in the tabloids with equal doses of salaciousness and prurience. When, years later, more transgender/non-binary voices began to make themselves heard, their listeners' only frame of reference, if any, was the sensationalist reporting of a prior era. Little wonder then that "gender people," to use a phrase coined by one of my former therapists, have struggled to find themselves understood, and even, too often, have struggled to stay alive.

In 2008, when I began my own transition, there were very few sources of information for people who needed help to heal the wounds of their personal gender struggles. Aside from case studies and other articles written by medical and mental health professionals, there were a handful of autobiographies written by people who had been through gender transition and lived to tell the tale. Such was the extent of the available literature back then, although the information available on the internet was growing exponentially at the time.

Tragically, as far as I know, back then there were few, if any resources for the spouses, partners, family, friends or employers of such individuals, and they are still very few and far between. I well-remember the impact my decision to transition had upon the people closest to me. My decision disrupted their lives profoundly, and I will never forget that the process of my own healing led to so many sad goodbyes.

In this book Ann Anderson Evans has made an important contribution to redressing the imbalance of information available to those whose loved ones reveal a side of themselves that they never knew about. Thousands of wives and partners will find similarities in Ann's story and their own, including the same unanswered questions.

Why did I not know about this beforehand? What could I have done differently? How long had my spouse/partner been this way, and why? What else is there to know that I don't know and may never know? In most cases the answers to these questions are unsatisfactory at best or left unanswered at worst. Nevertheless, these questions need to be asked, and this book does us all a favor by asking them.

Ann's narrative also opens a window for everyone into the personal struggles of "gender people," and the impact their struggles have on their intimate relationships. Sadly, Terry's actions and inactions were typical for a person struggling with gender identity issues, especially a person of Terry's generation; e.g., the hidden store of opposite gender clothing—my guess is that, as a young person, Terry may have cross-dressed using his mother's wardrobe when she was not home, and this carried over into his adult life in his choice of secret clothing—a reluctance to share or discuss what is really going on inside their heads, among other similarities. These behaviors are a cry for professional help that is rarely sought and often unavailable.

In reading Ann's narrative, I felt sad that Ann wonders whether she might have done more to help save Terry's life. It is a shame that many survivors of others' suicide experience similar feelings of responsibility or guilt.

In Terry's case, my own experience of the shame that our society and culture inflict upon transgender people makes me believe that he, too, was unable to overcome the shame that accompanied who he was. I remember sharing with my own mother at the tender age of seven my desire to be a girl, and being scolded so harshly that it would be fifty years before I could bring myself to share it with anyone else again, including several therapists. If Terry had had a similar experience, and this book suggests that he may well have, I feel sure that whatever Ann did or didn't do it would not have changed the outcome.

This book gives me hope that the ability of transgender and cisgender people to communicate with one another is not forever lost.

Rev. Terry Cummings
West Hartford, Connecticut
August 2023

Rev. Terry Cummings was ordained as a Unitarian Universalist minister in 2018 after a long career as an attorney in New York City. She is a member of the transgender community. She is currently working on a novel based on her experiences in ministry and lives in West Hartford, Connecticut.

Chapter 1
Terry Leaves

I never worried that Terry would leave me. Having married in our sixties, we felt we'd captured an unexpected shower of fairy dust. For all our fourteen years together, we frequently joined hands for a warm, smiling moment. We were so lucky to have each other!

But one night, he did leave me. He placed a plastic bag over his head. The thin kind used to bag vegetables in the grocery store.

I woke early and he wasn't there, so I went into his office and at first saw only the back of his head, which had something on it. He was sitting upright in the upholstered light green armchair, his arms relaxed on the arm rests, his legs splayed. *He probably fell asleep there*, I thought. But something was wrong. Circling around him, I saw a band of plastic lying on his neck, and a thin layer of plastic sucked into his mouth. *Huh. I always thought people died because they couldn't inhale, but this suggests it was because he couldn't exhale. How interesting.*

His expression was at rest, normal, only dead.

I took a step backward.

"Terry! What have you done?"

He had never failed to answer me.

I lifted the bag from his face to touch his forehead. *Maybe he's still alive, or recently alive. Has he gotten out of bed early to do this, or did he do it last night?*

Cold as marble. His skin was shiny like marble, too.

I started toward the bedroom to get my cellphone, careening down the hallway like a clown, shaking from head to toe.

9-1-1 would want to know what had happened. What had happened?

They took my name and location and asked if I could meet the EMTs in the street.

"Yes."

Should I greet them in my nightgown? Put on a bathrobe? How can I dress myself when I'm shaking so? Should I bother with underwear? I took undies from the drawer, a bra was lying on the dresser, and I put on the first top I encountered in the closet, and the first pair of pants, slipped into sandals and went out to stand on the front porch. *What should I tell them?* He'd cried uncontrollably the night before after watching a documentary about Lance Armstrong.

"I can see why they banned him," he could barely get the words out, "but why for life? Never to compete again? He was the most beautiful athlete I've ever seen."

I'd embraced him, he'd calmed down, and I went to bed.

I was half-asleep when he came to say goodnight, as he always did, turned down his side of the bed and put his CPAP machine in place. Then he came around to my side. But he didn't kiss me, as he usually did, he stood there with a supernova smile.

"What's up with you?" I asked.

The intense smile was unusual.

He said, "Goodnight."

Is this what I should tell them? Should I tell them that he said he'd prefer to choose the moment of his exit from this world? What did they need to know? What should I do now? Can I get into his computer? Do I have enough money to live on? We'd only moved to this house two months before and I didn't know the neighbors. *Who must I tell? Who could come help me?* My daughter was in Buenos Aires, my son in San Francisco. *I can't drive in this condition.*

I was on the porch when the regimented, kindly EMTs arrived five minutes later. *Have I dressed correctly? Have I forgotten something? Am I wearing underwear? Do my colors match? Do I look odd? Do I somehow still have my nightgown on?*

We went into the office where Terry was, or wasn't, and one of the EMTs placed a black box on the floor and attached sensors to Terry's chest.

I was confused. "Why are you doing that? He's stone cold. He's dead."

"We're required to do this," he said, concentrating on the flat line. He put the sensors on another part of Terry's chest and got the same result, so he turned to his partner and nodded his head, then put his equipment back in the box.

I wandered into the living room and sat on the light green couch that matched the chair where the matter that used to be Terry was. Out the window, I saw a police car pull up and two officers got out. *What will the neighbors think? Will they think their new neighbors have brought a curse on the neighborhood? Maybe they won't see.* It was 5:30 in the morning.

The officers stood as sentinels in my living room, directing the traffic and explaining procedures. The coroner, a middle-aged, pleasant woman with gear and cargo pants, arrived, greeted me, went into the room where what used to be Terry and the EMTs were, and closed the door. I didn't ask what they were going to do. Terry wasn't mine anymore.

Another policeman arrived, who introduced himself as "the detective." His name was Rosario, though I didn't know whether that was his first or last name. Rosario is an unusual name in white-bread Vermont. The life Terry and I had lived until three months ago was in Hoboken, where people spoke Spanish in the elevator, and Russian, and Creole, and everything else. I wanted to say something to him in Spanish, but there was no Spanish in Rutland, Vermont. People were moving to Vermont to escape the virus, but we'd bought the house in December, when the virus was a distant pulse from China. It would be too defensive if I explained that. I didn't want to feel like a foreigner. Rosario might not want to help me if I tried to speak Spanish. He might not speak Spanish. As he turned to go into the room with the EMTs and the coroner's assistant, a meek, short man in dark clothes came in the door.

"Hello, Mrs. Stoeckert."

I never go by that name, but since Terry's last name was Stoeckert, it was a good try.

"I'm the chaplain."

"Oh, hello. Have a seat."

He took off his baseball cap and sat in a chair across from me.

"What church do you serve?"

"I'm a local Christian pastor."

A Christian pastor? An evangelical? Terry was an atheist. I'm a Buddhist. Is he going to tell me, or be thinking, that God will send Terry to hell for the sin of suicide the same way he thought I'd go to hell for having had an abortion? To him, we're both murderers, unless he does some fancy finessing. I should be kind to him, but how can he impose the burden of courtesy on me at this tender moment!

"I'm here if you want to talk."

His presence brought forth memories of unhelpful sanctimony that I had fled from. *He's come like a vulture to the death feast. Is he going to pray? I bet he's got a Bible in his pocket. I should make him feel valuable.* He radiated the certainty and false humility of the Pharisee. *He's a kind man, trying to help. Terry would be appalled but nice. I must be nice, but I must also be true. Maybe this is a moment for truth.*

He cocked his head slightly forward, righteous, inviting a response. He smiled slightly, but his eyes told me he was just doing his duty. *Poor guy got dragged out of bed.*

I felt an elegant poise, not affected by circumstance, invulnerable to punishment. *What worse can happen to me?* I sat back quietly, my hands folded in my lap. "I want to tell you that what you preach about suicide causes desperate people to feel ashamed and guilty instead of giving them solace and healing. People like Terry, who are in some kind of agony, are criticized and reviled, and I don't thank you for that."

"We all have our different faiths," he mumbled. I wasn't sure he'd understood what I'd said because I expected a substantive reply. There was powerful emotion in the room and he remained in the shallows. *God damn!* "Your faith makes people feel like shit. Sorry to say that, but I'm feeling very frank right now. Today is like the Apocalypse when all is revealed."

He turned his baseball cap in his hands. "I'm here to help, if I can."

He's just in the way. I retreated into the good manners suitable to superficial encounters.

"Thanks for your good thoughts."

I didn't care what he thought, but I was conscious of the policemen. *What is the proper behavior in this circumstance? If I don't cry, will they think I didn't love Terry? Should I cry a little just to put all these people at ease, so they won't think I'm crazy?*

"How do people usually act when someone kills himself?" I asked the two policemen standing guard over me.

The older one took the lead in answering.

"Oh, all kinds of ways. Some people are numb and some are hysterical."

"Does it happen often?"

They both nodded yes.

"Fairly often, yes," the younger one said. "Yesterday we were at the house of a young man, 25 years old, with two children. Overdosed. He'd been clean for two years."

That's depressing. Imagine. I didn't know what to think about Terry's suicide. Maybe momentary despair took a wrong turn. Maybe he didn't intend suicide. The band of plastic like a necklace around his neck confused me. *Does that mean he'd tried to pull off the plastic bag? No, that couldn't be right. The bag was torn off downward, to keep it ON his head.* I couldn't find a place for that in my mind. It would sit there until I could comprehend it.

I wouldn't know how to kill myself, but in the aftermath of Terry's death, my soul felt less tethered to its mortal coil. Connection to my body was dissolving. My hands moved without telling them to. Tears flowed from my eyes without a push from my heart. *Does this mean I'm dying? Shouldn't I be going with him? We did things together. We are, were, TerryandAnn, AnnandTerry.*

I wept softly, moaned a little, while the two policemen stood silent guard.

Rosario came out of the death room and sat at the other end of the comfortable green couch. The chaplain had somehow disappeared.

Tears were seeping out of my eyes, and I kept wiping them away with a Kleenex. I had taken Terry's cellphone and wallet with me into the living room, and Rosario asked permission to look at them. He produced his own cellphone and took pictures of everything in the wallet; the two-dollar bill he always carried, the lottery tickets, his license, credit cards, even the cash.

I knew the password to get into Terry's phone, and Rosario took pictures of its screens. He asked what medications Terry had been taking, and I led him to the bathroom where he took pictures of the medicine bottles. The medicine in the bottles had kept him healthy, but now it had nowhere to go. I picked up one of the bottles and turned it round and round. *Should I throw it away?* It was now no more than a notion. *It has lost its purpose. Have I lost mine?*

"Are you his wife?"

"How long have you been married?"

"Did you find him?"

"Has he ever tried this before?"

"Do you know at what time he did this?"

Then Rosario looked away and said, "I'm sorry I have to ask you this, but," he turned back to me, "did he have any history of interest in asphyxiation for sexual gratification?"

This interview is turning into standup comedy. I leaned back on the couch and laughed. How absurd that would be! It took me a minute to focus on an answer. "I don't think so. I mean…" I turned my head from side to side, "…uhhhhh, if he did, I didn't know about it."

Rosario waited a moment before asking, "Have you ever hurt him or wanted to hurt him? Did you know anybody else who might have wanted to hurt him?"

This was the first moment that grief stabbed me. It pierced my heart and the blood coursed out. My mouth was open and I couldn't close it. I would have fallen to my knees if I'd been standing up.

"No!" *Why had he hurt himself? What had it felt like to die? Surely he was very sorry to leave me.* "Never. I would never hurt Terry." When I think of my own death, I think of the people I will miss. My strength was ebbing. It was hard to talk.

"I know it's difficult," Rosario was squinting as if in pain, "but you have to understand, every suicide is considered a crime scene."

This was an unexpected turn of the wringer, but instead of making me weaker, it woke me up. I took several long breaths and summoned some of the defiance I'd felt toward the chaplain. My brain was beginning to kick in. "Dealing with a suicide is complex, but being a murder suspect adds an intriguing new layer of complexity."

Rosario laughed. "You're not a suspect."

"I'm feeling a sudden pang of compassion for people who are suspects when they might not have done it."

My mind was inching up to the surface.

Rosario took Terry's cellphone, promising to give it back soon. I explained that all our business dealings were done through Terry's cellphone since we'd just moved here and hadn't changed all of our accounts. But Rosario insisted. They wanted to see who he'd been talking to.

A grief counselor snuck in at some point, an overweight middle-aged woman of benevolent mien. I was glad to see her. She could help me walk across the room, which seemed impossible at that point and didn't seem to be part of the policemen's assignment. "Do you want to be here when they take Terry away?" she asked.

"No. I don't want to remember him that way," I said, and she took my elbow as we walked across the kitchen and into my office. I took the blood pressure machine out of the drawer, 135/105. The 105 was a signal that I was under pressure. I had to calm myself down. I had an odd feeling that if I was going to follow Terry into death, it would happen as a kind of ascension—I didn't want to have a stroke or a heart attack. That would be so bourgeois.

I sat in my office chair with my elbows on the armrests and my hands intertwined over my chest. I didn't want to hear the rustling, the doors closing, the mumblings of the EMTs or the clicks of the stretcher as they took the heavy body out of the house. Terry weighed around 250 pounds and moving him would require some engineering.

I burbled on about how I'd found him and he'd mentioned suicide but I never thought he'd do it that night and we were happy together and I'd just moved here and didn't know anybody and I wasn't sure what I'd do now. I didn't stop burbling until I was sure they'd moved Terry out.

I'd never had to handle suicide before, so I approached it from every direction in hopes that the grief counselor would give me some interesting, useful information. Maybe something about how or why people succumb to suicide or about how people handle suicide or how common or uncommon it is or how people don't just up and kill themselves, or do they? But she just listened. And then they were all gone. I hoped I wouldn't regret avoiding Terry's corpse. I didn't want to stamp his cold forehead and unresponsive hand into my senses, into my dreams.

Now I was alone, and I went through the sun porch into my backyard. We'd moved into the house in March and hadn't yet witnessed spring there. In our Hoboken apartment, chives were the only plant that survived on the windswept balcony; they played dead in winter then pushed up green sprouts every spring. In Vermont, there were a few daffodils, masses of light blue forget-me-nots, red buds on the wild apple tree, and plants I was waiting to identify.

The classic tropes about impermanence and the cycles of life resonated in my addled brain. I would need to be reborn now, joining the natural forms that come alive in spring.

This little shot of hope lifted my spirits a little, and I turned to phoning the people who needed to know: our best friends, my daughter in Buenos Aires, and my son in San Francisco. He had been living on the West Coast for years, and I felt out of touch, so when he said, "I'll be there tomorrow," I was confused.

"How can you do that?"

"Wait a sec while I look up the flights." I could hear his fingers tapping the keys of his computer.

"Uh, I think I can get a flight that will bring me into Albany around two o'clock."

As I went to sleep that night, I listened to the silence. There were no traffic sounds, only the gentle soughing of trees and an occasional announcement from a nocturnal bird. I wanted to be here, away from the sirens and horns of the city, where I could feel spring and sleep in peace.

When my son pulled into the driveway in his rental car the next day, it was the coming of a karmic angel, a bright cloak of salvation. He guided me through the next week, taking me for walks like the family dog, and when he left, I could walk across the room, drive the car, and remember my passwords.

***

Over the next few weeks, I settled into a new routine, but thought about why Terry had done it. COVID cut him off from his daily activities, and we'd postponed our plan to spend a week every month or so in our apartment in Hoboken because New York was the epicenter of coronavirus infection and Vermont had almost none. But people don't end their lives because they can't watch the New York Knicks play basketball or go to their favorite restaurant.

I phoned an old friend, Rita Kaehler, a retired psychiatric social worker. I like her because she is ruthlessly truthful, innovative about how to solve problems, and loving but unsentimental. I felt hesitant to intrude into her professional space, so was relieved when she encouraged me to tell her what had happened.

"Okay," I said.

"Let's follow the breadcrumbs," she said.

Chapter 2
Ann Meets Terry

We met in December 2006, just as I was closing out my accounts on Match.com and other dating sites. Over the last three years, I'd read the profiles of hundreds of men, had countless email correspondences, phone calls, and a few affairs, but now there was only a pile of good-byes, and I was exhausted.

Except for Marty, a tax lawyer who lived on the Upper East Side in a white apartment with original Picassos and Renoirs on the wall. Every Thursday night I took the bus into New York to spend the night with him. He was a methodical person, and we had a strict schedule. I arrived, he ordered dinner from a nice restaurant, it was delivered, we ate, had sex, watched the Mets or *Sex in the City*, had sex again, slept, woke up to his alarm at 6:30, had sex, then I strolled through Central Park and down to Port Authority, took the bus, and arrived at my house in Montclair for breakfast. Marty was a niche boyfriend, and that felt like enough.

When I started to date again in 2003, I hadn't so much as held a man's hand for twelve years and had no intention of marrying again. I didn't trust myself to choose wisely, and didn't think I would be a good catch, myself. I was 61 at the time (and everybody knows men like younger women), had a track record of marital failure, and my two children had also suffered from the dramas in our household and struggled sometimes. A wise man would think twice about marriage to a woman like me. Marty's world and mine intersected only on Thursday, and it consisted only of the two of us. He wasn't interested in my past.

Before pushing the button to sign off the last dating site in December 2006, I saw Terry's photo. He seemed kind, not full of himself, intelligent, so I dashed off a note: *We're both college professors, which doesn't guarantee that we have anything in common, but it might be interesting to find out.*

In our first phone call, Terry said that I'd been "at the top of my to-do list." I would have heard from him the next day. Our mutual attraction was an omen.

Though I had written to him first, he grabbed the lead, calling me every day. If I wasn't home, he chatted with my daughter—I appreciated his strategy of approaching me through the most beloved corridors of my heart. We each had plans over the Christmas holidays and for several weeks we got to know each other only over the phone. He had an easy laugh, a nice voice, and a relaxed attitude toward life.

Every man I had encountered on the phone, by email, or on the internet over the previous three years began with sex. They went through a callous, horny patch at the beginning. I diagnosed this behavior as a test to see whether they would be rejected, a kind of performance anxiety. Most women shut men off at that point, but I rode through it, unless they were too disgusting, until the respectful conversation began. Once over the rough beginning, I got to hear about their lives. A friend said that "Affairs are not about sex, they're about conversation."

Terry was the only man I can think of who didn't do that. He didn't throw out insinuations, ask questions about my body, complain of being rejected by a wife or lover, or otherwise test the sexual waters. I gave him high marks for humanity.

From his profile, I knew quite a few things about him. His name was Terence Michael Stoeckert, he was 63, never married, no children, raised in Queens, lived in Hoboken, taught Economics and Finance at Stevens Institute of Technology, also in Hoboken. A Google search revealed he'd been Teacher of the Year more than once—a reassuring recommendation.

Men who live in New York City won't cross the Hudson River even for sex, but Hoboken was on the Jersey side of the river. He called it "one of New York's nicer neighborhoods." The flip little joke implied that living anywhere but New York City was somehow second-class.

After the holiday season was over, he suggested we meet at The Nook, a restaurant on 9th Avenue in New York. If you can meet in the city, why would anybody want to meet anywhere else? I was used to the New York superciliousness, though it always annoyed me.

I also lived in a New Jersey town, Montclair. It was far enough away from the city that I didn't have to worry about being hit by a brick falling from a scaffold, squashed by a collapsing crane, or run over by a delivery person going the wrong way on a one-way street. On the way to meet a friend for lunch, I didn't have to dread an unexpected parade, construction delay, or transit breakdown. Nevertheless, I enjoyed going into exciting, eclectic New York and accepted Terry's invitation without comment.

"Drive in. You'll find a parking spot," he said, as if there existed a magic parking spot finder. The holiday season was over and parking spaces would probably be easy to find, so I did drive, but that evening, they were fixing water mains and 10th Avenue was blocked down the middle, with fencing, cones, flags, and construction workers protecting long digging machines. I turned into 46th Street, forgetting that this was Restaurant Row where double parked cars sludged up my progress.

My annoyance grew as I cruised the streets, squinting to read the parking signs. "Park Here for 20 Minutes from 2–4 Except on Tuesday and Never On Weekends" with 'And Only If I Say So' in little print near the bottom. When I found a space, I wrote down the location because nothing will take the buzz off a good time faster than forgetting which street your car is parked on.

I stood in front of the restaurant, wrapping my coat close as I tried to calm down and warm up. It wasn't fair to be cross with Terry just because I was cross with myself. It was I who had decided to waste time in search of Prince Charming.

The pavement had shifted over the years, had cracked, been repaired, and was graying from rain and dirt. A parking meter slumped toward the street. An old lady wearing a headscarf like the ones Queen Elizabeth used to wear rolled her crackling shopping cart past me; a tricked-out clown with a red bulb on his/her nose leaped into the street to hail a cab; tired office workers trudged home.

I saw him coming, crossing diagonally against the light. He had an unpretentious way of walking, canted a bit forward, feet a bit splayed, arms swinging freely at his sides. He was a big man, wearing black pants, white sneakers, and a dark green zippered jacket with a couple of inches of ribbing above which rested a mound of tummy. His hair was gray-white and raggedy.

He was tall enough that I could lay my head on his shoulder; I liked that very much.

I reached my hand to shake his; he took it and placed his other hand on top of mine, squeezing gently. Such a generous greeting. He wasn't handsome, but he had a lovely smile and a warm manner. The Nook was full, so he took me up the street to Rosa Mexicana.

Conversation came easy. His eyes engaged with mine without flickering to the side to watch people coming past our table. I liked that. He was paying attention.

He was amused when I told him I had to write down the street where I'd left my car. He was a numbers person, while I was a words person to whom the numbers on New York streets all look the same. We were White, he of Irish, I of Welsh heritage. We'd been raised in religious households and then rejected the religion; for him, Catholicism, for me, Christian Science. Our mothers had both been reluctant housewives who went out to work after their children were grown; his mother worked in the accounting department of American Airlines, and after my father died, my mother got her college degree at 60, and became the first female councilperson in Montclair. I was a writer; he was a reader. We both liked to cook, eat, and drink wine.

"But here we are drinking beer," he teased. "Goes with the guacamole."

"Livin' the high life," I said. "When I was raising my children our big night out was Friendly's. If we were lucky, I could afford sundaes for dessert."

I offered to split the bill, but he refused. He was behaving by the rules we'd both lived by in high school—the boy paid for the entertainment. The price paid by girls for that gesture was decades of cooking and cleaning the house. But in the moment, his gesture held an old-fashioned grace.

I wanted to see him again, but didn't want to compete for the bill next time, so I moved the venue. "If I can't share the bill, I will be forced to offer you a meal cooked in my own kitchen." Our negotiation felt organic, natural, as it should be. Terry wasn't sexy, but he was curious and kind. He wasn't going to hurt me.

By mid-February, he was spending weekends at my house.

But why give up Thursday nights with Marty?

During my Hedonistic Period I'd experimented with telling the truth. I was trying to keep as few secrets as possible. What pleasure is there in pretending that the world is other than it is?

If a man asked if I was dating other men, and I was, I told him the truth. Until I entered into an agreement of some sort, I considered myself free to do as I wished with no explanations. I couldn't afford to spend another decade in a misguided relationship. Besides, the girl-claiming practices which were common when I was a young woman seemed outdated.

Terry called one Thursday night at 9:00, my night with Marty, and left a message. Not being home at that hour suggested I was out somewhere, and he deserved a version of the truth to explain why. I told him I was in the habit of meeting with an old beau on Thursdays—the word 'meeting' was vague enough. I told Marty that from now on I couldn't spend the night because I had a boyfriend.

Chapter 3
A Birthday Holiday

For my 64th birthday at the end of February, Terry took me back to Rosa Mexicana. He wasn't goopy, but he did sweet things for me. I kvelled when I referred to Rosa Mexicana as 'our restaurant'.

Over the pre-prandial margarita he said, "During dessert I'll tell you what your birthday present is." I forget everybody's birthday, and was not used to having others remember mine, so I felt like a ten-year-old when I learned he had a present for me.

I had a present for him, too, not for any occasion, just for fun. Once, he'd hooked his finger over the lacy part of the fanciest undies I owned and said, "I like this," so I got a fancier set of bra and panties to surprise him with. Its lace was itchy and the bones were digging into my ribs, but it was my birthday! While we waited for the guacamole, I asked, "Do you want to see my new bra?"

Terry broke into a smile. "Of course."

I folded back the edge of my blouse to show him the lacey band at the top of the bra without noticing that the waiter had arrived at the table. He couldn't suppress a small smile, and I gloated. Terry and I were not going to be cowed into acting our age.

After we ordered dessert, I asked, "So what's my present?"

He wagged his finger. "I said 'during dessert,' not 'when we order dessert'."

"Oh, come on. I'm so curious. Is it bigger than a breadbox?"

"It has no size at all."

"No size. Huh." I wrinkled my brow. "Is it a ticket?"

"You might say that."

"A theater ticket?"

"No."

"Let's see, a parking ticket, a ticket to ride…is it a plane ticket?"

"It begins with a plane ticket." He paused for effect. "Tell me anywhere in the world and I'll take you there for two weeks."

Terry, a *deus ex machina* fallen unexpectedly from the sky, was offering to raise me up and take me to…where?

This was a chance to visit a place I wouldn't ordinarily consider. Australia came to mind, the homeland of my first husband. My children had Australian passports. It was part of my life, though I'd never been there. But it was so far away, and going to my first husband's homeland didn't sound so romantic. Japan, China, India, Vietnam, and Bali were also far away. Mexico might be nice, but Terry didn't speak Spanish, so I wouldn't be able to either, which would be frustrating. I'd already visited London, Paris, Rome, Vienna, Madrid, Israel, and Turkey. Scandinavia would be interesting, we could take a cruise that stopped in St. Petersburg, Helsinki, Stockholm, Copenhagen, and Oslo…too much work.

I chose Hawaii, the epitome of all things carefree and optional. What an audacious birthday present! I had, however, been trained by experience to doubt. So many men had said, "Let's get together soon," and you never heard from them again! Terry had created a titillating dessert show at Rosa Mexicana, but would he really take me to Hawaii?

He came through, the first of many times I would affirm that he meant what he said. He spent hours researching B&Bs and islands, and planned a trip based around Kauai. He liked my choice. He'd visited Hawaii many years before, just after he got his pilot's license, and had flown over many of the islands, so he knew his way around. It was delicious knowing that he wasn't just throwing a gift on the table; he was working to make it truly delightful.

I told Marty I'd be gone for a couple of weeks.

I recognized Terry's anxiety as we climbed into the taxi for the airport— had he remembered the tickets, had he brought his laptop? A few years earlier, I'd taken my two teenage kids to Europe: the rental car broke down, I ran out of money on my credit card, and we lived on bread for our last few days in Paris. Now someone else was doing the worrying. All I had to do was pack my own stuff and get in the car.

My pleasure in Hawaii was not the tropical fruits, yacking birds, and enveloping sea, it was knowing that someone was taking care of me.

Terry was a great planner, but he needed a Firebird to inject excitement and challenge. My job was to think up some adventures. At our B&B in Kauai, I suggested a naked caper in the hot tub. Terry worried somebody might see us, and I answered, "So what?" He was hesitant, but I insisted.

"Come on. You'll love it."

In the soft Hawaiian night, he took off his clothes with his back to me and slipped quickly into the hot tub so his rolls of fat and private parts were under water. He was fat, that is true, and nobody would say the dimples in his behind were attractive, but every part of him was becoming dear to me.

In the hot tub, we shared our virginity stories. I lost mine at 17 after a hardware salesman from Tennessee proposed marriage. He left the next day and I never heard from him again. Terry didn't pop the cherry until he was 27 years old. A woman in a bar invited him to her place and he was still in her bed when he heard a car drive up and the woman said, "That's my boyfriend. You gotta get out of here." He grabbed his clothes and climbed out the window.

"Twenty-seven? How could you wait so long?" I asked him. "I would have tackled the postman."

He shrugged. "I've thought about that, and I think it's because I grew up in Catholic schools and they told us that girls didn't like sex. I guess I believed them. It always felt like I was pressuring them, or forcing them, and I didn't like that feeling."

"Damn the Catholic Church."

"It took me a long time to get over what I was raised with."

We lay back against the side of the hot tub and contemplated more stars than I had ever seen. "So beautiful. Thank you for bringing me here. It's the best birthday present ever." He took my hand under the water and we lolled in silence.

"What did your parents think of your apostasy?" I asked.

"My mother worried about my soul."

"She was devout, wasn't she?"

"She was, and Dad worked as the church custodian at St. Pancras in Queens. He had dinner most nights with the bishop."

"Why?"

"My mother made a decent pot roast and a pretty fair roast chicken, but the rest of her cooking was sandwiches and mushy peas. I have nothing bad to say about her, but she generally wasn't a good cook."

Our skin began to wrinkle, so we got dressed and sat on the broad *lanai*. Birds made an ungodly racket in the morning, but in the evening, their calls were quiet. The tiny Japanese housekeeper joined us, and she and Terry traded GO stories. He had brought a burnished wooden Japanese GO board and a set of smooth black and white GO stones to Montclair and was taking occasional private lessons with a GO master. Until I met Terry, I'd never heard of the game, so when we played, any hint of competition was ludicrous, but we had fun discovering how I would lose.

The two of them moved to a discussion about Japanese prints, and in a lapse in the conversation she looked over at me. "How long you been married?"

I was caught off guard by her question and didn't answer immediately.

"We're not married," Terry said.

"Why you not make honest woman of her?" the housekeeper said with a twinkle. "Why you not marry her?"

I was the object of their conversation, not a participant, and was glad I didn't have to answer.

"Did it ever occur to you that I'm not the one who doesn't want to get married?" Terry kept his eyes on the housekeeper, but I felt the comment was aimed at me.

His deft answer made me love and trust him more. He seemed to be suggesting that he'd been considering it, and it seemed that without my saying it, he sensed my hesitancy, my fear of marriage.

There was no hurry. I could think about it.

Chapter 4
Setting Up Shop

After we came back from Hawaii, he brought his desk and some clothes to Montclair but continued spending a night or two every week in Hoboken.

Our harmony wouldn't have been so sweet if I hadn't enjoyed the feral chase of football, the intricate geometry of basketball, the swift attack of hockey, and the grit and precision of tennis. Golf didn't interest me. All spring, Terry anticipated the Tour de France, his favorite sporting event.

"You might even find me awake at six for the Tour. Even five o'clock sometimes." That was dedication!

I cooked one night, he cleaned up, and the next night we switched roles. He focused on meat, with vegetables as an afterthought, often a simple salad. He'd learned techniques from his chef friends—preparing the *jus* for a roast or soaking potatoes for French Fries in vinegar. My style was more vegetable oriented, drawing on Adelle Davis, Julia Child, *The Joy of Cooking,* and ethnic cuisines.

During or after dinner each night, we watched at least part of a game, each sport in its season, unless we were binging *The Sopranos, The Wire, Deadwood,* or some other series. He was not fond of overdressed PBS period pieces or silly comedies, though his favorite movie was *Dr. Strangelove.* We watched all the Kurosawa/Mifune films. He loved Beckett, an Irishman who shared Terry's jaundiced view of the world. I had a more sprightly outlook. My favorite author was Henry James. I claimed that *Mary Poppins* was more than a frippery for children, and I could watch Fred Astaire for hours.

He felt there was a correct sexual schedule. If we didn't get around to it for a while, he acted as if we hadn't gone to church on the required number of sabbaths.

I would have liked him to display more of the standard male gambits, more take-control moves, more spontaneity. He was always trying to please me and I was always trying to excite him, and the impulses didn't match. My fancy underwear had evoked only a verbal response. I danced, flirted, fondled, and teased, which he enjoyed, but no roaring urgency came back at me. He never rejected affection and was endlessly tender. He was sensual in his affections and I thrived on the warmth and closeness. It was a different kind of loving, and maybe this was the proper mix for older people. His sexual potency was attenuated and he took male hormones and Cialis, but isn't that what happened to most older men? The bottle of hormones next to his razor had dire warnings about what would happen if a woman touched it.

I'd been on a wild dating ride for three years, now maybe I was gaining the proper perspective.

During our pillow talk one night, I said, "We're wonderful at intimacy, not so great at sex." He smiled and gave me a squeeze.

I weighed sex, in whatever guise, against the kindness and caring, reliability, amusement, safety, and stability of our relationship. A sexual partner could always be found through the internet, but comforting qualities are rare, so I honored and treasured them. Comparison of Terry with Marty revealed a blatant irony; Marty was all sex, Terry was all love. How ironic that I might have to give up one for the other.

My social life was centered around the Unitarian-Universalist congregation in Montclair. One of the members offered to share her enthusiasm for country dancing during a fundraising evening. Bringing Terry into that circle, where I'd been known as a single woman for years, felt exhilarating. And if he could dance, even a little bit, it would be wonderful. Moving in rhythm with another person, challenging each other by subtle moves and countermoves, reacting together to music thrilled me.

"Is it in the church?" he asked.

"It has nothing to do with religion. It's just dancing."

"I don't like going into churches."

I didn't want to argue about churches, but I also didn't want to miss this dance. It had been many years since I had done any kind of dancing with a partner. "When did your church allergy begin?" I asked.

"I remember the exact moment. I was in fifth grade and I asked one of the Brothers what people did in Heaven and he said they passed their days in glorious contemplation of God's greatness. That sounded more nearly like Hell to me."

I burst out laughing. "But you continued in Catholic schools after that."

"They weren't so bad. But I skipped mass on Sunday most of the time. I'd come home and my mother would ask me the subject of the homily and I'd make something up. I think she knew I hadn't really gone."

"I always went to church with my parents."

"Maybe they went on Saturday, I don't remember. My father was the church custodian so maybe he was working on Sunday mornings. I don't remember why, but I was always supposed to go on my own. So let me turn the question back to you. Is there a moment you remember?"

"Oh yeah. When the Dean of Women at Principia College told me to read the chapter on Marriage in *Science & Health* and one of the first paragraphs started, 'Chastity is the cement of civilization.' That's just ridiculous. I closed that book and haven't opened it since."

"Somehow, I don't think that Christian Science was quite as oppressive as Catholicism. Anyway, the minute I walk through a church door, I feel like I'm suffocating."

"There won't be anything church-y about it. We'll just be dancing."

He sighed and didn't answer for a few seconds. "I'll give it a try, but I'm a terrible dancer."

"You're an economist. You can count to four, or in the case of a waltz, to three, can't you?"

"In theory only."

"It's not *Swan Lake*."

"Okay, you asked for it," he said.

I put on my swirly skirt and off we went.

The pews of the sanctuary were cleared to the side, leaving a long hall for dancing, and we sashayed around as commanded. Terry didn't naturally move in rhythm. He bounced up and down instead of back and forth. I imagined the thought "I'm a terrible dancer" blazing through his head, which hampered his movements worse than the lack of rhythm in his bones.

Toward the end of the evening, there was a moment for social dancing and I grasped it lustily. Men are supposed to lead, but he didn't take to that, so I pushed and pulled him left and right, round and round, and finally, I bent backward into the crook of his arm for a dip. His arm gave way and I collapsed onto the floor, where I lay laughing out loud until he leaned over and took my elbow to help me up.

I embraced him and put my head on his shoulder. "Okay. You *are* a terrible dancer."

Chapter 5
The Loyal Troop

One of Terry's oldest friends was Sherryl Feinstein. They had met as graduate students at The New School and enjoyed intellectual parrying and soirées with fellow philosophizers. When I met him, Sherryl's health was failing after many years of treatment for cancer, and I met her only a few times, the last of which was in the hospital a few days before her death. There was only one chair next to her bed and Terry sat in it while I stood on the other side. The lighting made all of us look ill. There were three other patients in her room, but they were either asleep or watching television.

Sherryl turned to Terry with an impish smile. "Where will you spread my ashes, dear?"

"Where would you like to make your last stand? Near Staten Island, maybe? I could sprinkle them from the ferry."

"Too Republican. I might wash up on the Statue of Liberty, which wouldn't be so bad, but I'd rather a place with no significance, just a natural place, someplace open." She smiled. "Not your bathtub."

Sherryl's ashes arrived at our apartment ten days later. Terry mumbled about renting a boat and going out in the bay, but for the moment, he stashed them in a bookcase.

I was touched by Terry's loyalty to Sherryl through her years of difficult treatments. He didn't toy with people. If we stayed together, he would be loyal to me, too. He was at my side, on my side. I would try to live my life in a sound manner, but if I was stupid, if I betrayed his trust somehow, if I got angry or decided I didn't want to do the dishes that night or ever again, if my breasts became lifeless slabs, my hair went gray, if I was employed, unemployed, yearned for beets and artichokes, folded my underwear wrong, even if I stopped loving him, he would be there.

After our trip to Hawaii, I met more of Terry's friends at a dinner in a private room at the three-star restaurant Picholine near Lincoln Center. Terry parked the car at Port Authority and we walked up. The spring air caressed us and the blooming street trees near Central Park displayed colors and textures as varied and exciting as any country glen. We held hands, then put our arms around each other's waist, then separated, then held hands again. Whenever we were together, we sought each other's touch.

Terry and one or another of these friends had shared apartments, been at each other's weddings, baptisms, and the funerals of their loved ones, caroused over world-class wines, taken road trips in the Arizona desert and the Valley of the Loire. Terry may not have had children, but that didn't mean he was alone in the world; this was his equivalent of family. They were Michael and Marybeth, Ed, Ralph, and Peter. Michael and Marybeth had a restaurant in New Jersey. Ralph, Ed, and Peter B. were single, but in different ways.

Ralph was a brilliant mathematician and Stevens professor, divorced with two children and some grandchildren. Ed was a retired high school Math teacher, divorced and starkly alone, an Eeyore sort of person. Peter lived a monkish life devoted to opera, the Catholic Church, his Differential Equations students at Stevens Institute, and fine dining. I was hoping I would be sufficiently entertaining and did my best to at least look good with a slinky black jumpsuit, my grandmother's pearls, pearl earrings, and makeup.

When we arrived, they were reminiscing about great dinners in their past, including which wine had been served—I was astonished that they remembered the vintage, the importer, the vineyard, the *terroir*. This group knew the difference between an *amuse bouche* and an *entremets*. I could fake it for a while, but had only one pertinent credential—my 'Italian family', of which I'd been an honorary member for forty years, owned a vineyard in Tuscany, and I'd spent a lot of time there. I waited for the right moment to slip this fact into the conversation.

I'd eaten at great restaurants, but always as a tourist, a one-shot visitor. At Picholine, we were given lavish treatment because of Peter B., who ate there at least once a month during the opera season. The staff knew him as an epicure and wine connoisseur. Between courses the chef, Terrance Brennan, came in to say hello.

Our 'white before dinner' was a Bordeaux, Corton-Charlemagne, and after one sip I realized what the connoisseurs were talking about. The full-bodied aroma was more like an aura, a layered, developing taste pleased from tongue to tummy. Was there a touch of peach? I giggled as I gave my novice opinion of the wine, though I figured I could catch a whiff of cherries or the barnyard as well as anyone.

"Corton-Charlemagne." Terry held up his glass to the light. "It will go well with my dinner."

"What are you having, Terry?" Michael asked. "I'm going with the duck."

"Sole. It's said to be imported from England."

"I didn't know you were into sole food?" Ralph was prone to puns.

Terry turned to him with a playful frown. "That was pretty weak, Ralph. I think you're floundering."

"Grooaaannn," I said. "How the mighty have fallen!" I draped myself against the back of my chair.

After we finished the main course, there was silence among the sated and woozy company.

"Did you hear the one about the monks in the monastery?" Terry said.

"Oh no! Here we go!" Marybeth slapped her palm to her forehead.

"They observe perfect silence," Terry went on, "except for one night a year when they gather at the refectory table and one monk, only one monk, is allowed to speak. The first monk stands and says, 'I think the morning gruel is disgusting,' and sits back down. The next year a second monk stands and says, 'I quite like the morning gruel.' Another silent year passes and on the appointed evening, a third monk rises to speak. 'I can't stand this constant arguing!'"

I couldn't stop laughing. It was bottled up joy and fun, amazement that I was listening to lame jokes in the private basement room of Picholine, friends with the chef, drinking the best wines in the world, eating debatably the best food in the richest city in the world, in the company of a kid from Queens. I joked, "Now I know why I chose Terry."

Terry's friends seemed happy for him and accepted me by default. I could relax.

Though Ralph was raunchy, Peter B. was a tad too delicate, Ed was gloomy, and Michael and Marybeth were too busy to be frequently available, these were my new friends. I was as obliged to like them as Terry was obliged to like my children. And they weren't half bad.

Chapter 6
The Past Intrudes

When we met, Terry had been living for forty-plus years in a rent-controlled apartment in Hoboken directly across the park from Stevens Institute, where he taught. He hated the fol-de-rol of being on the regular faculty and was an adjunct. He'd abandoned his Ph.D. because one mentor died, one moved away, and the last one didn't approve of his thesis.

"But I'm making more money now than most Ph.D.'s. I've been lucky," he said.

He lauded the view from his 18th floor apartment. "Until they built the W Hotel, I could see from the George Washington Bridge to the Verrazano Narrows Bridge. You'd pay millions for this apartment on the New York side of the river."

"How much do you pay for it?"

"A little over a thousand a month. Utilities included."

"Wow. I pay eighteen thousand a year just for property taxes."

If we settled down together, it wouldn't make sense to keep both the apartment and my Montclair house, but such thoughts were premature. We'd only been together for a few months and there was still a lot to learn about each other. I chided myself for continually measuring the relationship against the possibility of marriage. Not seeking marriage was liberating, but the old Cinderella, happy-ending pattern of thinking was ingrained in me.

Financial considerations brought discipline to my expectations—if we were to pool our financial resources, I'd want to see that my children were protected. We were in our sixties and it would be foolish not to acknowledge that we were in the last act of our lives. It would be foolish to keep my house just so I had a place of my own.

He had shared the apartment for eleven years with Joan, a brittle, brilliant, unwell Renaissance figure who'd entered Harvard at 16. They'd broken up contentiously two years before, she'd left most of her belongings in the apartment, and I was in no hurry to become familiar with Joan's belongings. Terry said she was now living with friends in New Jersey after a mental health crisis. When the crisis passed, she'd come for her things.

Considering that I was still seeing Marty every Thursday night, I didn't want to get into a conversation about other relationships. Resolution of this was Terry's problem and until he resolved it, I saw no reason to visit the apartment. But one time he was at Stevens for a meeting and we had tickets for a play at St. Ann's Warehouse in Brooklyn, so it made sense to meet him there.

I took the train to Hoboken, left the station, and walked along the lovely river promenade. The pier from where my great-uncle had shipped out to the First World War was still there, transformed into a park.

Terry's 25-story white-ish building had nothing to recommend it other than its location, one block in from the river. Terry buzzed me in and I took the elevator to the 18th floor, where he was standing in the hallway waiting for me. In front of the elevator, there was a stretch of beige linoleum and beyond that thin blue carpeting with small red flowers stretching to the right and left, clean and utilitarian. Rent-controlled. What did I expect? It was a good deal.

I remember the next moments from the inside, from my heart. Terry steps back, I walk in, and my heart drops. A cheap white stove and refrigerator stand on a linoleum floor in the kitchen. Beyond the kitchen, I see the dining room table covered with newspapers and books in dense disarray, lit by a naked light bulb hanging from the ceiling.

I go into the living room and I'm…the right word is 'appalled'. Lamps with disconnected wires. Metal file cabinets. Things I suppose are sculptures. A couch covered with too much stuff to sit on. The unobstructed view of the Hudson River and the New York skyline are beautiful, but looking at a beautiful view cannot overcome an ugly room.

I'm thinking of the last two years with my first husband Ernest when we lived in a house that was even dumpier than this apartment. Over a couple of years, he tore the place apart. I was ashamed that my kids came home to this but had to wait until I got permission from the Court to leave. My heart's still banging with the disgrace of it. Thump. Thump. Thump.

Funny thing is that more than most people, I know how a person can get trapped in such a mess. I feel sympathy for Terry. He's trying to pull himself out of this situation, like I did. He's found me. He's come to Montclair. He's still got his job. It's not easy.

Still…is this the wagon I want to hitch to?

Terry's observing my ill-concealed reaction. "Hugo had very avant-garde tastes."

"I would call it industrial. You only have two chairs at your dining room table. I guess you didn't have guests?"

"People stood." Terry's talking like this is normal.

"People ate their dinner standing up?" Surely feeding guests a dinner they had to eat standing up was awkward and uncomfortable.

"Nobody seemed to mind."

What planet does this man live on?

"We argued so much that we divided up the space. I worked in the dining area, and Hugo and the parrot were in the living room."

"The parrot?" I careen off into a new bizarre corner.

"We had two parrots, but they didn't get along so in the end we only had one."

"Where is the parrot now?"

"Texas."

I'm thinking I'm not living here. Never living here.

"Every time I asked Hugo to take his stuff—"

I've been confused, trying to make sense of this, then it strikes me. Hugo? "Who's Hugo?"

"Oh." He looks stricken. "I thought I'd told you."

"Who is he?" Is Terry homosexual, bisexual, or something?

"Hugo's Joan."

"What does that mean?" I can barely stand.

"Joan suffered gender dysphoria and she transitioned and became a man."

Poor Joan. Oh my. "How did that work out? Is she, or he, better now?"

"Emotionally, it has helped a lot, but he's still very sick." Silence falls.

Here I've been thinking I'm so strong, so reasonable, so experienced. Thinking I'd figured out the boy-girl thing, finally, and look what happens. I'm doomed to failure. Doomed to die alone. I'm caught in another trap where things look good, but underneath there's big trouble.

Terry's not abusive like Ernest, or manic-depressive like Tom. Two husbands. Three husbands? How could I even think of it? Sane and solvent, I say. I'll only consider a man who's sane and solvent. Solvent, check. Sane, I doubt it. I want to cry.

Terry looks like he's giving up, too. He turns around and sits down on one of the dining room chairs. "I felt a loyalty to him. Wanted to help him. We spent a long time together."

"I'm not living here."

"I wouldn't expect you to. Not the way it is."

I give a little laugh. "To put it mildly." I'm going to stand up for myself this time, not going to let any man drag me down. I'm 64 years old, don't have that many years left, and I'm not wasting them on some guy who can't get it together.

Terry gets up with a dead serious look and comes over to me. "I promise."

I snort.

He takes my shoulders and squeezes them. "Listen to me. I got myself stuck in a situation that's been hard to get out of, but I promise you. I promise you. From now on Hugo is not going to interfere in our relationship. I'm sorry I didn't handle this better. But I love you. I love you and you're not going to be in the middle of this ever again."

He looks pale, shaky, he doesn't want to lose me. I don't want to lose him either. He's going to fix this. If he doesn't, we're done. But I don't say this to Terry. We need to get out of there so I can settle down. "We'll be late for the theater. Let's go."

I couldn't parse how Hugo's experience reflected on Terry, other than that Terry had stuck with him as he went through the gender transition, and I already knew that Terry was a loyal, compassionate person.

Back in Montclair, New Jersey, where I felt at home, I got over my initial shock and confusion, I wanted to know more about Hugo. I didn't want my shock to be the last word about him and a few days later brought up the subject again. The weather was thick and foggy, and a fragrant chicken pot pie hit the spot. Terry matched it with a light *pinot noir*.

"I don't know what being transgender means. I've encountered a couple of people I think might have been transgender." I hesitated. I wanted to radiate openness about a subject I had a visceral negative reaction to. Intellectually, I was tolerant, but my body's cells had trouble obeying the command of my mind.

"Who do you know?" Terry picked up the wine bottle and re-upped my glass.

"There was a woman, I think a transgender woman, at a weekend workshop I went to. She was tall broad-shouldered, built like a man, but she had this tiny pocketbook hung over her arm like someone in a 1950s movie. I shied away from her."

Terry was relaxed, listening. He listened to me, and to everybody, by training his gaze directly on me.

"Go on. What did you think of her?"

"Listen." I spread my hands in the air, "I'm neutral regarding decisions like this that I know nothing about. I've been the odd-man-out too many times to judge others. I remember Christine Jorgensen. I was confused about her, but okay, she wanted to be a woman. I didn't know how they made that happen."

Terry nodded. "It's more than that. It's gender dysphoria." He spoke authoritatively, and he ought to know, having gone through this with Joan.

"I understand gender and dysphoria, but what does that mean in real life?"

"All her life Joan felt like a boy, but she didn't, or couldn't, do anything about it. She even got married, but they divorced. Then she started getting strange sicknesses. She'd lie all day on the couch with a fever and nobody could figure out why."

"What does that have to do with gender?"

"I'm not sure, but she felt that she couldn't live as a woman any more. It was eating at her."

This news made me squirm.

"Kind of literally."

"Right. Finally she found a doctor who could help her and she had the top operation." He seemed relieved to be telling me about Joan. "The bottom operation is a lot more difficult."

I sighed. "Huh. I admire you for sticking with her. Not many people would have done that, I guess. You're a wonderful person. But even knowing how hard it is, it still makes me uncomfortable. There was a visiting minister at our church who was transgender. I was sitting up front with the choir, so I was close to her. First of all, there's the instinctive mix-up. From the back, this is clearly a man—she made her transition at 52, so her body was fully formed as a man.

"This man turns around and there's this grinning woman with rouge on her cheeks, big hands, big feet. It messes with my antennae. It brings me face to face with all the subconscious ways I've been trained to behave, to react. Though I don't think it's training. It's just how I am."

I was afraid that being frank about my discomfort around transgender people would be interpreted as criticism of him, who had accustomed himself to Hugo. But there was nothing in his eyes to show uneasiness or disapproval, so I went on.

"She was giggling with the little children, though no woman I know acts that way with little children; it was as if she was acting the way men think women act, though women don't actually act that way. I found it kind of insulting. Do men think women are so silly and superficial? I thought that trope had disappeared a long time ago. It was as if a woman wanted to be a man so she cut off her hair, put on dungarees, and strode around barking at people. Do you know what I mean?"

He shrugged. "It's hard to change gender."

"I was so jiggled around in my reaction that I didn't go over and speak to her, though I admire her for taking her stand and know she must be going through a lot. It was as if negative magnetism was at work. I don't know how else to explain it." I stopped to think for a minute and Terry continued watching me, waiting. He'd said he liked "intellectual women," and it was refreshing to be able to think something through without feeling he would lose interest.

"You say that transgender people know since childhood that they're not like other people. It's not like they decide to change into women to annoy the rest of us. But if we are born with an inner gender identity, then what about the way I was born? I was born to sigh at broad shoulders, to love the rasp of a beard against my cheek. I like the sound of men's voices. So what about my natural tendencies that have also been there since I was a child, well, not the whiskers part. I was at least a teenager by the time I felt the rasp of whiskers." I stopped to smile and brushed my fingers against his cheek. He smiled.

"Just telling me that this particular set of manly shoulders, this deepish voice is a woman will not overcome my natural tendencies. When I saw that first trans woman, the one with the little purse, it was like my own attraction to her broad shoulders was punishing me. It's kind of hard to explain, much less to explain away."

Terry watched me until he realized I had nothing more to say. "You don't have to be around Hugo if you don't want to."

I gave a little laugh. "He's the other way around. Maybe from the back you'd think he was a woman and he'd turn out to be a man. I think I could handle that better because I'm not attracted to women."

"He's a small man, but I don't think you'd mistake him for a woman."

"The issue with Hugo is more than that. He sounds like trouble to me. According to you, your apartment is in the condition it's in because of Hugo, and you said he was mentally ill. I've lived with enough mentally ill people to last me for the rest of my life. There's so little I can do to help them. I don't want to be held responsible for another mentally ill person if I can help it."

The subject was dropped. Hugo was living in a different universe now and would not ruin my relationship with Terry.

The fact that, left on his own, Terry would live in squalor was more concerning.

During my Hedonistic Period, it was sometimes hard to keep the men I was meeting straight. Which one had a Dachshund, and was this the one whose daughter was a ballerina? I kept thinking I should have a database, but I didn't create one. I did use lists to turn animal attraction into an intellectual exercise. They helped keep me from being willful and impetuous.

With Terry, the honeymoon period was not devoted to blazing sex, but to sharing our thoughts and feelings without shame. Maybe this was how relationships between older people should develop, but I didn't have confidence in that conclusion, so I turned to a list as an outside referee.

Pros	**Cons**
Loyal to friends and to New York City	Not handsome
Includes my children w/o objection	No affinity for children in general
Self-sufficient	A loner
Professionally/financially stable	Procrastinates
Has never been married	Has never been married. Why?
No entanglements, no kids	Catholic childhood
Strong libido	Different sexually
Kind, patient, affectionate	Sometimes narrow-minded
Healthy	Hasn't gone to dentist in 25 years

Reliable, punctual, adaptable	Irish, blue-collar chip on shoulder
Supports my writing ambitions	Different artistic tastes
Exceptionally intelligent	Slow moving, defensive thinking
Good cook w/ different repertoire	Limited to meat, runny gravy
Has great wine collection	Doesn't like artichokes, cream sauces, beets
Plays the lottery	Plays the lottery
Wine/food connoisseur	Drinks a lot—likes pot
My friends like him very much	Enjoys company of difficult people
Smart sense of humor	Tells dumb jokes his father told
Evaluates people accurately	Shines only with close friends

If it had mattered only to me if I made another mistake in my choice of partner, I might not have been so prudent, but if our devotion continued to deepen, he would become part of my children's lives, too. He had been an only child, had no children of his own, and evinced little understanding of the condition known as parenthood, but his chats with my daughter when he first started calling me daily showed that he accepted my children as part of the package. The burden of choice still rested with me, and I couldn't afford to make another catastrophic one.

The negative and positive sides of my Terry list balanced out, perhaps tilting positive. Compared to Marty, he was an all-star.

Chapter 7
Austria

Austrian friends had invited me to visit them that July, and they were happy to include Terry. We flew to Vienna and by the end of our first evening it was clear that my friends enjoyed him and were happy for me. That meant a lot.

I never brought them presents; instead, I cooked for them. On our second day, Terry and I went to the high-end Viennese supermarket, Julius Meinl, and bought halibut, cream, a mix of mushrooms, asparagus, and butter. Terry spent easily a half hour chatting with the wine guy and chose two bottles of *sauvignon blanc,* champagne to go with home-made parmesan crackers before dinner, and a sweet German *Auslese* to go with the peach pie.

Making pies in Europe is a challenge because they have neither rolling pins nor pie plates. The measures are all in liters and grams and the oven temperatures are in Centigrade. I used a chilled wine bottle as a rolling pin, and a rectangular glass baking dish as a pie plate, and Terry calculated the translated amounts into grams. There are no standardized 'cups' or 'teaspoons' or 'tablespoons' so I used an ordinary spoon and measured by eye. That's not so hard for a pie because all you need is flour, sugar, and a little salt. The aesthetic of a round pie plate is lost. Our friends had spent time in the U.S. and knew what a pie was, but they weren't attached to the aesthetic of a wedged slice. Square servings were fine with them.

Terry wasn't bothered by jet lag, but I was, so I had to take a nap after we came home from our shopping trip so I'd be fresh enough to make the dinner, which was delicious; Terry made the fish dish and I prepared the rice, asparagus, and dessert.

It was a lovely evening, so we sat on the terrace, surrounded by our friends' expansive flower and vegetable garden, until after the sun went down over the crest of the hill above us.

I felt close to my friends and relieved that Terry fit in so well with them, and that Terry liked them so well. That night I slept soundly and long.

On our third day in Vienna, Terry and I strolled along the Graben. For lunch, we found a restaurant with outdoor tables sheltered on three sides by a six-foot privacy hedge. Our view out the open side captured all the charm Vienna could offer: ancient buildings, narrow cobblestone streets where Mozart used to walk, a brilliant sun cooled by a refreshing breeze.

We ordered our food and Terry sat back and casually said, "Well, I guess we could get married if you want. If you want."

After dropping that bomb, he paid me no attention. He looked around at the people passing by, turning his water glass around and around. It took a minute to convince myself that I'd heard him correctly.

I loved the man, and I trusted him. He'd kept every word he'd given me, beginning with Hawaii. He was wicked smart, professionally successful, and egalitarian in his treatment of others. He cared about my children. We got along smoothly.

He was not going to abuse me the way my first husband Ernest did; Terry was a kind and quiet man. He was not going to descend into profound mental illness the way my second husband Tom had; Terry was rock solid sane, a little eccentric, but sane. His deepest flaw was procrastination, but I'd known many people who procrastinated. He'd managed me masterfully, overcoming my fears, continuing at my side every day with reliable good humor, patience, and affection. I would not have been the one to propose marriage, but now that he mentioned it, I admired the unobtrusive way he had waited for the right moment.

I was suddenly tired of being the captain of the ship and surprisingly relieved at the prospect of relinquishing, or at least sharing, the helm. It required my giving up some of my own agency, but I would no longer bear the sole burden of every decision and risk. Terry wasn't perfect, but I wasn't perfect either. I couldn't ask him to take on my past, so full of crashes and mistakes, and my flaws without accepting that I had to also take on his. He planned our trips, our evenings at the theater or a jazz club. He kept the budget, researched investments, and did the shopping. I hate shopping. We shared cooking chores, but I did all the other household work. Outside of infrequent dinners with his close friends, I provided our social life, including this visit to Vienna. We had worked out our life together well.

Marrying Terry would also be good for my children. I would be financially secure and there would be someone to take care of me if I got sick. I'd have enough money to visit my children wherever they were. That consideration was important since my son and his family had moved to California.

Witnessing a stable, loving relationship like ours would provide a template for them that they had not seen in my other two marriages. If Terry died before me, there would be no legal questions about who was his heir—we were both in our 60s and it would be foolish not to think about such things—so none of his 50 or so cousins could suddenly appear out of the blue to claim first level kinship.

I had recently been pondering what to call him. 'Boyfriend' sounded juvenile, 'partner' required explanation, 'life partner' was arch. One friend introduced him as, 'Ann's gentleman caller', and I sympathized with the dilemma. There is a word for someone who held Terry's place in my life, 'husband'.

I found myself saying "We could have a helluva party." That evening, our hosts broke out the champagne.

Chapter 8
A Helluva Party

Back home, we booked the first available autumn Saturday at Michael and Marybeth's restaurant in Harding Township, New Jersey. I had a haunting premonition that Terry would die before we could get married. The chances were minute that this would happen, but it hung around, no matter how I tried and tried to talk myself out of it. My fears were neurotic—maybe I couldn't believe my good luck.

Terry survived, and on December 1st, 2007, fifty-two people took planes, trains, and automobiles to get there, and a new tribe was formed. A dozen of Terry's friends and colleagues came, and my family members ranged from my two-year-old grandson to 85-year-old aunt Jean.

My friend Carri flew in from Arizona to officiate.

This was a toy wedding compared to full-blown extravaganzas with the white gown where they said "with this ring I Thee wed." We were in the upstairs room of a restaurant, with dining chairs lined up in rows. The flowers were on a dresser that held the restaurant's tablecloths and silverware. The atmosphere was casual, amiable, and suitable for the joining of two people who'd already been through other relationships.

In his 30s, Terry had been engaged to Gretchen, who died of ovarian cancer. He said, "I was in a pretty deep funk for a long time after that." Then there was Joan, who became Hugo, and I don't know how many flings. I'd been married and divorced twice; lived without a man for twelve years, then rollicked through a Hedonistic Period. Both of us were, in other words, seasoned at navigating the rocky roads of romance and profoundly grateful to have found each other.

In my vows, I wanted to announce that I was not planning to become Mrs. Terence Stoeckert. I was anticipating a life of my own, even if I was married. This is what I came up with:

"For the last decade or so, I have been wondering if it is enough to live life alone."

Beginning last January, I found a new answer to that question.

I wouldn't want to give the impression that Terry and I are absolutely perfect together.

For example, we were discussing the music for the wedding, and I said, "What kind of music would you like?" and he answered, "The Grateful Dead."

But Terry is more perfect than I had thought I had the right to desire.

Now my vows to Terry.

I vow to always appreciate you; your kindness, vast compassion (he forgives me all the time), your intelligence, devotion, grace, humor, and all else.

I also vow to stray—outside the limits of dogma, tradition, and creed, into ever new territory, lest we get bored.

I love you, and I am delighted and proud to be your wife.

Terry's vows sounded flowery and archaic to me, almost pedestrian. "Ann, I will always love you, in sickness and health. I will protect and support you, shield you from harm. You are the love of my life, and I will love you always." He broadcast the miracle of what would become a beneficent marriage. He appended, "…and I promise that I will learn how to dance."

We left our guests and drove through a rainy late afternoon to the Mohonk Mountain House in New Paltz, New York for our honeymoon. Our room had a balcony, a stone fireplace, and a bed heaped high with warm bedding. I would have loved to tangle our naked bodies in front of the fire morning, noon, and night, but that wasn't his way. An orgy only lasted a few minutes; our relationship would last until one of us died. He was my true husband.

The lake and forest paths around the Mountain House were not of much use in December, but we walked where we could, had massages, and ate and drank nicely. There were no chores to do, nobody to call, no appointments, so we settled into one long conversation, mostly about our families. Terry's parents had died and his aunts, uncles, and cousins had either also died or had fallen out of touch. I was still interested in the people who had raised him.

Terry had already met my aunt Jean and my brothers and their families before the wedding, but that day he met cousins and their families, too. As we sat in front of a cozy fire, I asked him to tell me more about his family. "You haven't talked much about them," I said.

"I left behind all that life. I wasn't Catholic anymore and frankly, most of my cousins bored me. I never enjoyed the big family gatherings. And as you can imagine, they were big."

We had the whole day before us, and I nursed peppermint tea and stared at the changing patterns of the fire.

"I was born in Seattle," Terry said. "My mother was probably not married at the time."

"Wow. Nice Catholic girl gets in a fix."

"She might have been married, I don't know. Every time I asked her, she got terribly agitated. I didn't want to hurt her so I never probed any further."

"Do you know who your father is?"

"Paul O. McDonald. I don't know what happened to him. From the little I know, they made an agreement that he would never have anything to do with her or me."

I was squinting with sadness but didn't want to interrupt him.

"When I was eleven my dad said one day, 'Come on. We're going to Court to make this legal'."

I was losing the sense of what he was telling me. "What does that mean? Make what legal?"

"He said he was going to formally adopt me."

"Holy cow! Weren't you shocked?"

He looked out the window. It had begun lightly snowing. "I don't remember. I think I was surprised, but it didn't upset me much. He was the only father I knew and that wasn't going to change. I learned that day that I'd been born Michael Terence, but I'd always thought my name was Terence Michael. I much prefer Terence. It's an elegant name."

"Do you think they changed it so Paul would never find you?"

"I have no idea."

"What about schools? Didn't you have to show a document of some sort to go to school?"

"I don't think so. They always knew me as Terence Michael Stoeckert. They were Catholic schools and they knew my dad because he worked for the church so maybe they just let me in. I don't think they asked for documents in those days though."

"Something must have happened that prompted him to formally adopt you. Hard to imagine that you might never have known he wasn't your biological father."

"He never explained." Terry went on to tell me that his father pinched pennies ferociously. He thought it was because he was raised one of seven children during the depression and had never forgotten the poverty. "My dad played the lottery and had contacts at the stables who passed on their tips."

"Did that work? Was it that crooked?"

Terry laughed a little. "If anything, I underestimate how crooked it was. When I was in college and needed spending money, Dad passed those tips on to me and, wise ass that I was, I passed them to all my friends. We pulled in a fortune till Dad found out." He paused and rubbed his cheek. "I ruined his connections. I felt badly about that." He sighed. "I cost him a lot of money."

In the upright world of my family, nobody played the horses or the lottery. "I've always wondered why you play the lottery. It's an odd thing for an economist to do."

He shrugged. "You're playing against a stacked deck in the stock market, too."

After a chilly walk along the lakeside, I'd taken a hot bath and was wearing a warm terrycloth robe with a blanket draped over my legs. I didn't feel like leaving our comfortable armchairs to go to the dining room, so we ordered soup and sandwiches for lunch. Terry put another log on the fire and we continued our conversation.

I smiled at him. "What would you do with, say, a hundred million dollars?"

He brightened. "I've thought about that. Hugo gave me the idea. After putting aside some for myself, and you of course, and your kids, I'd establish a foundation that would seek out the oddballs, the misfits, the geniuses in the corner whose lack of social skills has disenfranchised them. So much talent is wasted because schmoozing is highly valued. The other possibility would be establishing a research foundation to study sensory loss in older people. Hearing, sight, even smell and taste."

"That's interesting. It'd be a lot of responsibility though."

He shrugged that off. "What would you do?"

"I'd figure out how much I'd need to live comfortably for the rest of my life, buy a house and so on, and endow my children with enough for them to live comfortably, then I'd give the rest away. I wouldn't want to have to keep track of that much money, and people would keep pestering me for donations. It would take some time to find the institutions or whatnot that I wanted to give it to. My former sister-in-law died young and left her millions to the Republican Party. I would not do that."

He laughed.

I was getting sleepy and took a nap while Terry read one of his science fiction books. I was always amazed how many hours he could sit in a chair reading without taking a break.

We had a partner massage later in the afternoon, and while we were relaxing in the sauna afterwards, I asked for more stories from his childhood.

"My mother tied me to a tree once."

"Really?"

"I wanted to see the rest of the neighborhood and I kept running away, so she tied me to a tree."

"How old were you?"

"I must have been about five. I've got a picture."

"I don't think I would've liked that."

"It didn't bother me particularly."

I reached under his towel and patted his leg. "However she did it, she turned out a wonderful man. And whaddayaknow, he's my husband!"

When we got back from our honeymoon, I called Marty to tell him I wouldn't be seeing him anymore. I'd hung onto him for longer than I should have because he was my last vestige of freedom.

He said, "You will be missed."

Chapter 9
Hoboken

Living together married felt different. We were building a life together.

His teaching schedule included a few evening classes every week, but on the other nights we played GO. I could see that he was making calculations that were more complex than my brain could handle. He dazzled his students by instantly calculating, say, the monthly payment on a 30-year $135,000 mortgage at 4.5 percent. I could figure it out, too, but it would take me longer and I would do it on paper, not in my head. My sensibly limited GO goal was to surprise him and throw him off his game.

Outside of our GO games, where there were no stakes, his decision making was slowed by the defenses he constructed. At every step, he stopped and looked around before moving forward. Was there something he hadn't thought of, was somebody watching him, competing with him? Was there a better, cheaper alternative? How would this decision look ten years from now? He wanted to be sure he'd thought of everything before moving ahead.

That would be good for me; I made decisions impulsively, on available evidence, instead of stepping back to think things through.

He'd gone against form where I was concerned—he made up his mind about me right away. I asked him how that miracle had happened and he said, "It sounds something like love." For all our differences of style and pace, we thought much alike. We both had an iconoclastic streak, though my iconoclasm was adventurous, carefree, sometimes heedless. Terry's was more cynical, anarchic, and calculated.

I teased him that he dressed like a homeless man; there were holes in his tee-shirts, he rarely got a haircut. When we went to the opera, he wore a shirt and sports jacket…and white sneakers. He'd learned his manners but did not judge others by theirs. He rooted for the underdog—the Dodgers, the

African-American, the Jew, the Native American, the Immigrant, the mentally ill, the gay and transgender. He was touched by the childhood memory of defending his Jewish neighbors against the slurs of his Catholic school classmates. He tagged their bigotry as a heavy count against the Catholic church, because his teachers allowed the ugly thoughts and words to stand without objection.

I was Terry's Firebird. I sang, I danced, I played the piano. I dressed up when we went out. I spoke many languages and had lived in many cultures. I was a college professor. I'd had two husbands. I had children. He delighted in showing me off, though I had never thought of myself as a beauty. When we went out, I did my best to look good.

When he took me to the Café Carlyle to see John Pizzarelli and Jessica Mulaskey, I donned a purple silk blouse and black accordion-pleated pants. I put up my hair and fussed over my makeup. I had my late Aunt Lillian's gigantic amethyst ring on my finger. When the doorman took the keys to park the car, he quipped, "Beauty and the beast." Terry was still laughing as we drove back home after the show.

I loved being loved for what I was. I didn't have to hold back. He indulged me, took care of me, protected me, and told me when I was going off the tracks. In other words, he did everything he had promised at our wedding, except learn to dance. He just didn't have the 1-2-3-4 (in the case of a waltz, the 1-2-3) in his system.

Bringing together all of our difference and sameness didn't take long. I could live without *Mary Poppins* and he could live without mysteries where people's heads got cut off.

Terry didn't mow lawns, weed gardens, or even notice maintenance issues. He was used to apartments where you called the handyman. Since I had to either take care of these chores myself or direct him how to do them (and he so profoundly did *not* want to do them), I began to think more positively about the Hoboken apartment. The numbers argued for a move. The annual $18,000 I was paying in Montclair property taxes could be used to travel. Besides visiting my son and grandkids in California, we planned to visit our Austrian friends every year.

Because of the financial crisis of 2008–2009, it took several years to sell my house. Terry used those years to meticulously plan for and execute a transformation of his apartment. It would have new floors, a new ceiling, freshly painted walls, and built in cabinetry. The dining room table I had grown up with didn't fit in the space, so I reluctantly sold it and we bought a new one from Amish carpenters. Terry made no plans to replace the naked light bulb hanging over it.

We produced some fancy dinners for that table, but guests either didn't notice the naked light bulb or were amused. He took a roguish pride in this marker of his renegade self.

My Montclair home was spacious and lovely, but in Hoboken my share of the rent was less than $800 every month, and my other living expenses were shared. There was enough money not only to travel and go to plays and concerts, but we could eat at the best restaurants. This was the right place to be.

The kitchen Terry designed was wonderful to work in. We had a Blue Star gas stove, a special German refrigerator that was narrow enough to fit into the required space, and black Silestone counters. My favorite feature was the pot rack. I could be working at the counter, turn around, and pull-down implements or pots, and likewise put them all away after they were washed but not necessarily dry. I had never worked in a more efficient kitchen.

The building was constructed as affordable housing in the 1970s, part of Lyndon Johnson's Great Society plan. By 2009, the plumbing was wearing out and the water was frequently shut off as they repaired a pipe, a drip, a mini-flood. Because of the poor plumbing, we couldn't have either a kitchen disposal or a dishwasher, so we had to wash dishes by hand. Terry enjoyed that and joked, "We have two dish washers." Ha-ha. The floors and ceilings were cement, so we couldn't have recessed lighting, and the wooden flooring was glued to the cement and some warping occurred. But we got what we were paying for and more.

There were two bedrooms, only one of which could be converted to a full office. Terry said I could choose where I wanted to work, but there was only one logical choice. His papers and projects were in a constant state of getting organized, and I didn't want his stuff all over the living room. So my office was a corner of the living room. We used Terry's office for extra storage of files and clothes, and it was our entertainment center, with a huge television on the wall. The better to watch basketball with. We adjourned there after dinner for our daily date. I had two dates during the entire span of my high school years and spent Saturday nights moping. It's silly, of course, but having a date every night felt like a delicious luxury.

Our habit of playing GO petered out. Either he was tired of playing with such an amateur, or he otherwise lost interest. Probably the latter, because he enjoyed curating our television watching.

A couple of times a week, we ate out. We might go into New York or to the Thai place, or Amanda's for the Early Bird special, or Court Street, or Cucharamama. Every day ended with fun and the pleasure of being together.

My corner 'office' received the direct beams from the morning sun, so I had to work with the blinds closed, or half closed, which canceled the beautiful view, but I wasn't watching the New York skyline when I was working anyway. It was worth opening the blinds every evening. The sun set in the west but its reflected rays burnished the New York skyscrapers with a different color every night—bright red and combinations that incorporated greens, golds, blues, reds, oranges, yellows, grays, and beiges in ever unique combinations.

My northern vista as I worked at my desk was the campus, from the Victorian Gothic stone building where the school was housed when it opened in 1870 to the modern glass towers of the Wesley J. Howe Center where Terry taught. Seeing this every day gave me a green, open feel. To the east was my unobstructed view of the Hudson River and the New York skyline.

If we had lived in an apartment among other apartment buildings, I would have felt cramped and citified.

On our first 4th of July in Hoboken, we invited friends to watch the fireworks in the Hudson River, right outside our window.

A couple of days a week, his teaching schedule took him across the street to Stevens Institute of Technology, where he taught in the business school. If I didn't have a class at Montclair State at the same time, I could kiss him good-bye, then go to the window and wait for him to appear eighteen floors below. He crossed the street onto the diagonal path crossing Stevens Park, past the playground, the dog run, the clubhouse for the baseball field, then he crossed the street onto the boulevard running a couple of blocks into the campus. I lost sight of him when he turned right behind the Babbio Center but could picture him in his classroom several minutes later.

I knew his walk from afar. I'd tuned to it from the first time I'd seen him coming against the light to meet me in New York: canted forward, feet a little splayed, purposeful.

The closer I could stay to him, the better I felt, and on days where he taught on campus, we were within touch of each other all day. That was the sweetest part of moving into the Hoboken apartment.

Chapter 10
What About Dying?

The program Terry taught in offered classes in other countries, and my own teaching schedule allowed me to accompany him for two weeks in the Dominican Republic. Two days before we came back home, he threw his back out while lifting a suitcase. For the flight home, United Airlines upgraded him to First Class so he could tolerate the flight. He was in such pain that he could not have tolerated sitting in Coach.

When we got home, he was diagnosed with sciatica. I brought Terry his meals and helped him get in and out of bed. We talked about what would have happened if he'd needed more care than I could give him, or if, in the future, one of us became gravely ill.

I said that I would hope to stay in the apartment, with a nurse, if necessary. I didn't want to go into an assisted living facility like the one my aunt Jean had recently moved into. The staff treated the residents like babies—"Shall we sing a little song now?"—and the food was crap.

"I prefer suicide," Terry said.

His blunt statement caught me off guard. I'd thought I was providing a realistic solution and here he was jumping off the deep end. "Lots of people say they intend to end their lives but most of them don't," I said.

"I've got a stash of pills in my drawer. Just in case."

"No! Don't take pills. They might not work and you could be brain dead for years."

He laughed. I was taking him seriously, but his levity suggested that he was playing with the idea.

"Okay. On the coldest day of the year, I'll hike to the top of a mountain and just never come back."

"With your sciatica, I doubt you'll ever climb to the top of a mountain."

"The sciatica will go away," he teased, "or I'll get physical therapy first."

"My mother's friend took a chair into her backyard on a frigid day and just sat there until she died."

"Smart woman," he said.

"Do you know that in the months between returning from Vienna and our wedding I kept having thoughts about you suddenly dropping dead before we could get married? It was stupid really. I don't know why."

He cocked his head in surprise. "You never told me that."

"You don't have thoughts like that, do you?"

"Nope. Never crossed my mind."

"I suppose it comes from being a parent. Parents are always thinking the worst is going to happen. But dropping dead is different from suicide. My father was a Christian Scientist and he didn't even see a doctor until four days before he died. You could say that he aided his own death by not asking for help. I didn't argue with him. It was his body, his life. But he was my father, not my husband. If you chose suicide, I couldn't bring myself to give you pills or an injection, I just couldn't do it, but I wouldn't stand in your way."

"Don't worry. I'm planning on living at least twenty years. That's not wishful thinking. Lots of people live into their eighties, why not us? We don't have to make my suicide plans quite yet."

"Right. Anticipatory grief is useless."

He looked at me for a little while, then said. "I hope you go first."

"Why?"

"Because I want to be there to take care of you."

The impact of this statement didn't hit me until the next day, and it fell deeper and deeper into me as time went by. It was the most romantic sentence he ever uttered.

Chapter 11
Stuff Under the Bed

When he got a little better, I brought the vacuum cleaner into the bedroom and reached the wand under the bed. I knew he had left boxes there, but had never been in the room with Terry when I bumped into them, so I took this chance to investigate. I pulled one of them out.

"What's this?"

Terry watched as I pulled off the top of the box and found a stash of women's clothes: plaids from the 1950s, psychedelic blouses with standup collars, polyester everywhere, frills and ribbons, and bows.

"Oh." I said and quickly put the top back on.

"I didn't mean you to find them this way," he reached down to push the box back under the bed. "It's nothing." He reacted like a man with a mistress who's trying to keep the letter in the lavender envelope with the flowery writing on it from his wife.

"Your reaction suggests that it isn't nothing," I said.

He sighed. "It's something I did. I don't do it anymore. I've never gone out in public dressed as a woman."

"You dressed like a woman?" I flinched thinking back to the remarks I'd made about men dressing like women.

He was found out and he didn't like it. He put his index finger on his lips, stared at the floor, and breathed. I sat on the chair next to his bed. I might just fall down as he told me the truth.

"But you don't like girly things," I said.

"What does that mean?"

"You know: applesauce, tapioca pudding, Oprah, ironed sheets, curtains."

"Ironed sheets! Don't you think that's a tad excessive?"

"Don't worry. I won't ever force you to sleep on bright, white, crisp sheets."

He laughed and shifted onto his back, fluffing the pillow under his head. "I don't think you have to like ironed sheets to have a well-developed feminine side."

"You have a feminine side. You're a nurturing person."

"I just don't like treacly."

"Like Mary Poppins."

"Exactly like *Mary Poppins*."

"There's a moral and ethical point in *Mary Poppins*."

He squirmed at the cock-eyed hope implied by my happy ending addiction, then changed the subject. "When I was a boy my mother dressed me up as a girl for Halloween, and the moment that dress slipped onto my body, I felt different. I liked it."

My brother had dressed as a girl for Halloween, too. Monty Python members were hilarious dressed as women. It was fun, funny. Terry was not thinking hilarious, though.

"It's nothing really. An experiment I run now and again."

I wasn't sure how to respond. If this six-foot, two-hundred-and-forty-pound man with a beard and size 15 shoes came tripping down the stairs in a dress and heels, my reaction would be to double up in uncontrollable laughter. Terry in lipstick would have zeroed out our sex life.

He was looking at the ceiling, and I was looking at him.

"I didn't think much of it, but years later, I must have been in my thirties, I had a girlfriend who wanted me to wear her panties. She didn't insist, she sort of dared me. And I liked it, so she gave me some more. Then a couple of years ago, I met this woman from Boston on the internet. She used to come down to New York to see me, and every time she'd bring clothes in my size. Shoes. Everything."

My heart was beating faster, my breath trying to catch up with it. I didn't want to make light of his experiences; I didn't want him to stop talking. "What happened to her?"

"She insisted that I go out in public that way, and I wouldn't do that."

I searched for a neutral response, something that would show him I wasn't going to leave him, that I loved him, that we all have our stories. After all, Marty, the embodiment of the discreet lawyer, was carrying on with his illegal immigrant Chinese manicurist who left her nightgown with roses on it in his closet. People are not always, maybe not ever, what they seem.

I stood up and pulled the vacuum cleaner away from the bed. "Women wear men's clothes all the time. My great-grandmother's photo was on the front page of the Brooklyn Eagle because she wore bloomers while riding a bicycle in Prospect Park. Scandalous! So it's not fair, right? Women can wear men's clothes but men can't wear women's clothes."

He had a way of studying my reaction whenever serious subjects came up, his eyes surveying me for signals while his mouth uttered ordinary words. "If it were simply a matter of logic."

Standing there beside the bed, holding the vacuum cleaner hose, a raging wave of anger came out of nowhere. I couldn't stop myself. "You know being a woman isn't wearing bras and high heels. There's a lot more to it. Being a woman means going to work in pain at least one day a month. It means coming home after a busy day and finding your husband and your kids playing games at their computers and nobody's thought about dinner, and your husband, I'm not talking about you, but lots of husbands, they look up and say, 'Oh! I'll go out and get something,' and that will just add 45 minutes to dinner and you're starving, so you have to go into the kitchen and make dinner or have a big argument. You've had a dozen arguments about things undone and you're in the position of accepting it or arguing all the time so you stop arguing and just do it, and that's partly your fault, because in the beginning you wanted to please him so you made him dinners, so of course he thinks you're the one who should cook dinner. You thought he'd step up when the time came, but he's oblivious." The more I talked the more I recalled. "And having men not talk to you about sports or politics, looking at you like you're a little girl. And men talking about how delicate women are when they're carrying the vacuum cleaner up three flights of stairs while eight months pregnant or stopping in the fields to give birth. What kind of women are they referring to? Women are not delicate and tender and scared and giggly. When there's a bombing, it's the women who pick up the babies before they run away. Maybe if a man was willing to *really* be a woman, to *really* suffer all the annoyance and indignities and resentment of being a woman, it would be easier to accept. But wearing women's clothes doesn't mean you're a woman, even if you have an operation that changes your body."

I ran out of breath and stopped talking. Terry stared at me.

"And to add insult to injury, here is a person who's dying to wear bras and girdles and high heels, all those things that most women are so damn glad they don't have to wear any more. It amazes me that someone who wanted to be a woman would not have noticed how happy women are that they don't have to dress like that anymore." I puffed out a gust of air, gave a little laugh and wiggled my shoulders. "Well! Sorry. Where did all that come from?" I gave a great sigh. "I guess I have to work on being more open to this."

"It's okay," Terry said.

"It is fun to wear costumes and pretend to be someone else, if that's all it means. Why is it all so dead serious?"

"It would get serious if I went down in the elevator dressed as a woman, except if it were Halloween," he said.

"I don't think you'd like the reactions. People would make jokes."

He rubbed his hand along his cheek. "We don't have to talk about it anymore."

Witnessing his discomfort made me fear for our relationship, so I had to make an effort to adjust. I gave myself little talks about how silly it was to be scared of a skirt but could not overcome my aversion.

It was a simple coincidence that around that time, we went to a play on Broadway starring Eddie Izzard, who is famously at least half woman. In his cameo scene he made the audience laugh until our stomachs hurt. His character was dressed like a man, but I had also laughed myself silly when I saw him on television dressed as a woman, or partly as a woman.

This was an opportunity to bring up the subject of cross-dressing again.

Our tributary joined the flood of people issuing from the theaters. Limousines, taxis, and beeping cars clogged the street, excited playgoers clutched their playbills, fans waited outside the stage doors.

I held tight to his hand so we wouldn't get separated. I had to hustle to be near enough for him to hear me. "Eddie Izzard makes me laugh harder than anyone except maybe Peter Sellers."

"He was good tonight," Terry said.

"And did you notice we were sitting two rows in front of Lauren Becall? She was one of my favorites."

Terry was plowing through the crowd, dragging me behind him.

"We should find some of his shows. Maybe there's a Netflix DVD or something."

"Hmmm."

"He cross-dresses, but he treats it more like a quirk than an existential storm."

Terry's attention turned to the web of crisscrossing traffic and the moment passed. I thought if we could approach this little by little, taming the spiders clinging to this subject, I might be able to handle him cross-dressing. Some humor and fun would soften my own transition to becoming the other half of a couple where gender was not stark.

But when Eddie Izzard had a show in New York and I asked Terry to get tickets, he didn't say no, he just didn't do it.

Chapter 12
Bang in the Night

In our first couple of years together, Terry and I were relieved and thrilled to have someone to sleep next to—we'd both slept alone for a long time. We snuggled close and repeated "I love you" and "I'm so grateful to have found you."

Then Terry's night terrors began. He woke up bellowing obscenities, threats, and emotions that I never saw in the day. "Get away from me, you sonofabitch. You can't come in! Don't point that at me! I said you can't come in!" His arms flailed powerfully, sometimes hitting me in the arm or the rib cage. His legs pumped frantically, wresting the sheets away.

I awakened when he sounded distressed, but didn't want to disturb his train of thought. In dreams people are working things out, and interrupting this process does not help them to do that. I woke him when he was over-agitated. "Terry! Terry! It's okay. You're okay." I stroked his shoulder and arm and held his hand tight.

He was dreaming that people were chasing him, locking him in a room, threatening him with a steel pole or a gun.

"Why do you think you're having these dreams?"

"I have no idea."

"Is there some childhood trauma or near miss? Were you bullied or humiliated or something?" I asked.

"I don't think so."

"They must come from somewhere. I never dream somebody is coming to kill me."

He squirmed and I stopped pressing. Whatever was lurking within him might have been hidden from him, too.

Sometimes he was convulsed with guffaws at clownish situations. He sang Irish songs and once he orated. "My children! I have gathered you together for this august occasion…"

I turned and watched this performance leaning on my elbow. "Terry!" I poked him.

"What was that!"

Laughter left over from his dream interrupted his answer. "I'm the bishop. Gathering my flock."

His past was full of bishops, an uncle who was close to the Pope, ceremonies, music, and vows made to a God he no longer believed in, though they remained in his brain's circulatory system.

The flinging arms were frequent enough that I took to facing away from him as I slept, reversing the habit of spooning that had so comforted us when we first got together.

A loud crash awakened me one night. He'd swept his arm out in self-defense and knocked over his bedside lamp. It wasn't broken, but its fall testified to the force of his terrors.

After that, I became more observant during the moments when I was awake and he was asleep.

He was going for countable seconds without breathing and I urged him to have it evaluated.

"Maybe you're having these night terrors because your body jumps into survival mode. With no oxygen for a while, it jumps into fear."

"I'm not breathing?" He was surprised.

"I timed it! You go ten seconds, maybe more, and it happens often."

He went thoughtful. "Hmmm."

"It's not good for you. Your sleep isn't deep enough."

In general, he hewed to an "I'm fine" attitude that smothered my infrequent supplications that he take better care of himself, but he must have been concerned that his outbursts would cause some real harm, either to me or the furniture, and he went to see Dr. DeMarco, a savvy provider who could swing with skeptical patients like Terry. He was a fine general practitioner whose cramped, dark waiting room was always stuffed with the indigent and the marginalized. Terry felt comfortable there.

He announced he'd be away for a night to have his sleep monitored, and I silently thanked Dr. DeMarco. The results diagnosed sleep apnea, and after he started using a CPAP machine, his sleep became calm and uninterrupted. I slept better, too.

He was otherwise gentle as a lamb, except when a driver wasn't behaving as he thought they should.

Chapter 13
Weighty Problems

Our first years together were Falstaffian, Rabelaisian, epicurean, indulgent, fun, and we both gained weight. I gained ten pounds but Terry gained forty. We ate healthy dinners, but he ate more, drank more, used more butter, ordered the double bacon cheeseburger with extra mayonnaise and butter, and snacked on ice cream.

Food was a central element of our lives. Besides eating out often, we both experimented with new recipes. Terry's specialized in steaks, chops, and seafood, while I excelled at soups, stews, sauces, crepes, soufflés, and dessert.

He was four inches taller than I and weighed over a hundred pounds more. That couldn't be healthy. Could it? At his fattest, he couldn't reach his feet to tie his shoelaces; he had to sit down and pull his foot over his knee, or put his foot up on a chair.

It deflated him to go into a clothing store where even the XXL didn't button properly across his middle, but refused to visit a 'big and tall' store. He kept clothes in our storage unit for each of his weight phases. He was never again going to wear that pair of skinny checkered tan pants from the 1960s, but he couldn't bring himself to throw them away.

When his weight shot all the way up to 280 pounds, I was concerned, but there was nothing I could say to him that I hadn't already said, no information in my possession that he didn't already have. He didn't need to be reminded that he wasn't getting any exercise. Nagging does not become any relationship and remarking on his lassitude would only make him feel more guilty.

He claimed that some external factor caused his weight problem: the removal of his tonsils as a child, medical tests that showed a slow metabolism, a thyroid deficiency, exercise facilities were too expensive or too far away, the sciatica would recur, or the right tai chi teacher had retired. He didn't utilize his membership in a local gym. He refused therapeutical assistance for cross-dressing, weight gain, even sciatica.

The fatter he got, the more he gave up, but the solution had to come from within him, and it seemed to me that there were tectonic forces shifting in there. I thought his outlook might improve now that he was getting a good night's sleep. When he found a compatible physical therapist, at least his fears about his back receded.

I told him, with a kiss, "I don't care how fat you are. It's your body, you can do with it as you choose. You're just as cute to me."

My sincere disinterest in his weight confused him. I wanted him to deal with it as a health problem, not as a judgment on his worth. His health was good. He was rarely sick, his blood pressure was normal, and his cholesterol was under 200—I needed medication to match his lipid profile. He had a heart condition that was under control and didn't limit him in any way.

Chapter 14
Whipping Boy

We were busy that winter. He was teaching four evening classes, and I had a daytime schedule at Montclair State University. We passed each other as we came and went, worked in our separate spaces in the daytime, and met when we could for our nightly dates.

One morning he came into the living room where I was working and said, "We need to talk." He walked over to the dining room table and set up his laptop.

"I need some help." I assumed it had something to do with the household budget, or he wanted my opinion on which shows to get tickets for.

He showed me an Excel chart containing columns of numbers on the computer screen.

The print was small and I couldn't read it from behind his chair.

"What do you want me to do?"

"I'm not losing weight. I'm at 281. I've tried everything and nothing's working. It's making me kind of panicked."

I recoiled. "I'm not responsible for your weight. I don't want to be in charge of it."

He sat back in his chair and looked downward, defeated. "I can't do it alone."

"Why not?"

His voice was so low I could barely hear it. "You know that all my life I've struggled with this. I gain, I lose then I gain again."

I'd set an upper limit of 160 for my weight. I was having too much fun eating at fine restaurants and had let it rise a bit. I weighed myself a few times a week, and if I was inching upward, I cut back on my eating. It wasn't easy, but it was simple. Why couldn't Terry do the same thing?

"Why don't you see an expert about this? Somebody who knows what to do. I don't want this responsibility."

He frowned, irritated. "I've been to a lot of doctors, and one of them gave me Fenfen, which fucked up my heart. I don't have much trust in weight loss doctors."

"What about a group? Weight Watchers or something."

"You know that sort of thing doesn't work with me."

I sat back and folded my arms. "What do you want me to do?" I could have said it more kindly.

He leaped into answering the question he'd been waiting for. "Let me show you." He clicked on the spreadsheet. "I need some kind of punishment if I don't make my weight. See, every Thursday," he pointed to a highlighted column, "I have to have lost half a pound. If I do that for a year, I'll have lost 26 pounds. I'll lose slowly and then I'll be able to keep it off. Maybe it should be two-thirds of a pound, or maybe even a pound. As long as I keep losing. It just has to be something permanent."

I sighed. "What about holidays or vacations or if you get sick or something?"

"Then you'll have to decide."

"Me?"

"The whole point is that I don't have the discipline to do this." His face was reddening.

"I don't want to be thinking about this all the time, worrying about whether you've eaten this or that, keeping tabs on everything you do. It makes me angry just thinking about it." I got up and took the two steps into the kitchen to put on some water for tea.

He was gauging my actions carefully. "Just Thursday. That's the only day you have to think about it."

My stomach was in turmoil.

"Just for a while, till I get this under control. I need some sharp discipline."

"Sharp discipline?"

"Yes. That's the point." He had a hangdog, defeated expression, though that doesn't convey the strangeness of it. "I need you to spank me."

I was turning on the gas under the kettle and turned to him in alarm. "What?"

"I know it sounds kinky, but I think if I know that if I don't lose the weight, I'll get a punishment, I'll keep it under control. You'd only have to do it once or twice. Just thinking about it would be enough to stop me."

I came back to the table and stared at the chart, feeling I was in another world "Oh my god. I've never done anything like this."

"It isn't as if you were abusing me. If I don't do something, I'll just keep gaining weight. You'll be doing me a favor."

"What do you mean if *you* do something?"

"I know. I know. It's asking a lot, but lots of people do things like this. It's very common."

I wasn't thinking he was crazy or weird, just that I didn't want to do this. "What's the end point? At what point will you be able to relax?"

"I've thought about that." He'd been doing his usual thorough analysis. "Let's say I lose 30 pounds a year. In two years that's 60 pounds, I'll be at, say, 220. But I want to get back to 190."

"One ninety will be unsustainable. You're a big man."

"Maybe, but I want to try."

I was at a disadvantage because he had thought this plan through and had it covered from every angle. I knew people who had permanently changed their body shape. It was possible. But what about the discipline issue?

Seeing my malaise, he struck a reassuring tone. "We'll re-evaluate as we go along. Every Thursday."

"I'll dread Thursdays."

"I think that after I've had this treatment a couple of times you won't have to worry about it. I just need to get turned around."

I was so roiled! Many of the men I had communicated with in my Hedonistic Period had a bit of S&M in them. Kinks were so common that I came to expect them: anal sex, exhibitionism, obsession over their mother, wearing ladies' underwear, group sex, bondage…there seemed no end to them. These men were telling me their stories on the phone or in emails, sometimes in person. When they found someone who would listen without berating them or hanging up, they felt free to make their confessions. A friend had told me to make my dating 'a research project', and nothing could have been more fascinating than seeing behind all those normal-looking profiles on match.com. I never had to meet the men in person so I listened and learned.

But this proposal unseated me. I sat at the table and rested my forehead in my hand. The tea kettle whistled but I couldn't move. Terry watched me.

I finally got my tea and came back with the warm mug in hand.

"It's such a little thing," he urged. "Can't you do this one thing for me?"

Maybe it would work. Maybe this was what he needed. Don't you do things like this for a person you love? There's a multi-million-dollar industry built around people who do this sort of thing. Could I do it?

"Okay. I'll try it. But I don't like it."

"You'll feel better when you see how it works."

The program was to begin with a baseline treatment that Thursday. He fashioned a homemade leather switch that I received into my hand. My arm was leaden and at first I couldn't hit him hard, but he explained that unless it hurt, it wasn't going to work, so I did the best I could, with every cell rebelling. His skin turned red.

I felt appalled that I had hurt him, and in counterpoint, angry and guilty that I couldn't execute this harmless ritual for him. But the act itself and the anticipation of another episode lay heavily on me.

It worked. For the next six months, he consistently lost weight every week, so I only had to do it once. I was happy for him and reclaimed the space in my brain that he had reserved for his visits to the scales.

Again, I admired Terry for his strategy. He'd calculated that if he told me about his kink before we were married, I might seek another man, and he was right. My aversion to hurting someone I loved was so profound, and my underlying tenuousness toward marriage so fragile that I would have continued with Marty. That would have been enough.

Terry never said as much, but I've concluded that he hoped having a secure relationship would make his cravings disappear, and I'd never have to find out about them. He was a daily partner without equal: kind, considerate, clever, fun. Besides dealing with the finances, curating our entertainment and travel, and doing the shopping, he anticipated my needs, supported my writing projects, deployed his considerable intelligence in my interest, amused me, tenderly held me, cooked for me every other night, and stood ready if I needed him. Terry gambled that our deep and loving relationship would overcome any shock I might feel.

I plumbed myself for unrevealed secrets equal to his but found myself unencumbered.

Theoretically, the Missionary Position was fine with me.

As time went by, Terry's proclivities became familiar companions. They were notional anyway, because I never saw him dressed as a woman and only had to flay him once. Besides, how awful were these kinks? I might have to discipline him once a year, and how distressing could cross dressing be? Arab, Chinese, Persian, Indian and African men wore flowing robes, I envisioned Scrooge in his white nightshirt. Western conventions restricted men to such narrow choices of dress! Wearing flowing clothes, or silks, or bows, doesn't harm anybody.

I suggested that he search for a group of men who liked to cross-dress, or maybe he'd like to join the Halloween parade in Greenwich Village dressed as a woman. He frowned at me.

I held up one of my nightgowns and said, "Would you like to wear this?" He turned it over in his hands, held it up front and back, and put it on without a word. Seeing him in the plain, long, dark blue nightgown was okay.

He wore it until the next laundry day, then went back to sleeping in his underwear. He said cross dressing was not a big part of his life. He said he didn't need it.

Chapter 15
Halcyon Days

By the time we met our Austrian friends in Provence that summer he had lost thirty pounds. Photos show him with a fresh haircut, wearing a handsome new sports jacket. Losing the weight made him proud and happy.

Our friends had rented a house surrounded by vineyards in Cucurron, in the Luberon region of Provence. Terry and I flew to Nice, and rented a car, driving up narrower and narrower roads as we got closer and closer to the house. We had to pay close attention to signs so as not to get lost.

I needed at least one day to recover from jet lag, though Terry was unaffected. The ancient stone rooms, high-ceilinged for coolness, had been renovated with modern conveniences, and we swam in the pool on a terrace.

The next day Terry and I and our Austrian friends drove to Marseilles where we enjoyed the art museum and bought soap. We needed to take a trolley, or was it a bus, to get to the museum. When we got to our stop, I was the last of my friends to make my way down the aisle among the standees.

A middle-aged man stood aside to let me pass, and cupped his hand over my breast as I did. That was a surprise. I had to hustle to join my friends, and didn't think to stop and punch him in the nose; besides, why bother. Wolfgang had waited for me as the others started down the street and I told him, "A man grabbed my breast. What man grabs old ladies' breasts?" I treated it as comedy.

Wolfgang was attentive. "That's not right. I'm sorry that happened."

I started to laugh. Wolfgang maintained his beneficent expression, but slowly dissolved into laughter, too.

"Maybe I have a future in France," I joked.

Our friends came to Provence every year and they introduced us to the greengrocer, the baker, and the butcher in the village. They knew the owner of the restaurant where we stopped for lunch.

As usual, I didn't get to speak much French. Our Austrian friends' English was close to native, so it would have been a burden on them if I wanted to practice my German. When my mother and I visited France in the 1960s, we spoke English in the hotels, but while we were buying bread, tomato, and cheese for a mid-day picnic or visiting a castle, or walked around town, we couldn't expect people to speak English, so I got an occasional chance to speak French. But to really speak a language, you need to be immersed in it for weeks or months, and I'd never had that opportunity.

Now, many years later, the French spoke English better than I spoke French. They'd been watching *Law and Order*, *Friends*, or the nightly news in English and had a command of everyday idioms. In one shop in Cucurron, I started speaking French and the salesperson threw her arms in the air and said, "You are American! I was one year in Sheecahgoh!" In order to switch to French, I'd have to quip back, but I hadn't spoken it in many years. My ear needed time to become attuned, and my mouth muscles had to loosen up. I acceded to the inevitable and spoke English. With one exception.

One evening we went to a restaurant in an old stone building on a slanting cobblestone street. Our family-style table was in a nook partially divided from the rest of the restaurant by a stone arch.

On this visit, my gift to my friends was musical. I played a Chopin waltz one year, made a CD of lullabies when their daughter was born, and this year I'd been taking singing lessons and was ready to sing some Schubert, in German.

We only had two more days there, so I was searching for an appropriate moment for my little concert. As we were waiting for our dessert, the place was emptying out, so I wouldn't interrupt anyone's dinner.

"I haven't found a time to sing my song for you," I said.

"Sing it now!" They chorused.

Without warming up, I wouldn't have the confidence to hit the required high F, so I adjourned to the ladies' room for some humming and arpeggios. I gave myself a little talk as well.

You have to sing full out. If you make a mistake, it'll be fine. Our friends won't care, and you'll never see any of the other people out there again.

I did some final breathing exercises and went back to the table. I aimed the song at the mural above our table. "Du bist mein Seele, du mein Herz…" Out of the corner of my eye, I saw the white jacket of the chef leaning against the door jamb watching me with his arms crossed. I sailed through the high F and came to the diminuendo at the end. "…mein bess'res Ich."

Some passersby on the sidewalk outside the restaurant joined the chef, the waiters, and our friends in applause. This was as close to grand opera as I would ever get, and Terry was beaming. He didn't know from Schubert, but his presence gave me the nerve to sing it.

Day by day, we were building up a store of memories like that one. We became annandterry, terryandann. His well upholstered shoulder was my refuge, his girth reassuring. I could no longer imagine cleaving to a man as skinny as Marty. His voice was a clarion, there was a heft to the space around me, something to reach out to, a gentle leash when I went briefly mad, bought something I couldn't afford, blamed others for my own unhappiness, or even turned for a sparking moment against him.

In such a case, sometimes centered around the damn naked light bulb above the dining room table or the disordered newspapers, he took the blow and after I simmered down, said, "I don't think you meant to speak like that," and I deflated, made an extra dinner, apologized, atoned.

My other two marriages had quickly become burdens, and it took time to appreciate that weight was lifted, not added, with Terry. It wasn't perfect, it required compromise and a certain measure of sacrifice, but this was a real marriage.

Chapter 16
Hurricane Sandy

On October 29, 2012, Hurricane Sandy arrived in Hoboken. The weather reports had gotten a few previous storms wrong, all that hysteria for nothing much; nevertheless, I went through the motions of bringing inside the two heavy stone monastery sculptures, the two brooms, the pot with soil and a spade, and the box holding the chives. I checked the back of the closet for the gallon jugs of drinking water, plugged the bathtub, and ran the water until it was full. I filled the largest bowls we had in the kitchen with water and found several flashlights and lay them where we could easily find them. Terry set up some candles.

The hurricane arrived on time, but the roaring winds, buffered by well insulated windows, did not alarm us. We were used to high winds barreling down the Hudson River corridor and crashing into our northeast corner balcony, or pounding in from the West. They were so strong that I couldn't grow anything but chives on my balcony.

It felt like a Snow Day, and we made it special. I'd gone through blizzards and hurricanes alone, and it was so much better to have someone to share it with, someone warm to sleep next to while the wind howled outside.

Over a steak dinner, we indulged in a Chateau Picon-Longueville, Red Bordeaux 1999. It tasted extra delicious because we were living outside of our daily world.

Terry told about where he was for another New York catastrophe, 9/11. "I stood on the balcony and watched the towers collapsing. It was a strange feeling. I wanted to do something to help, but there was nothing to do. I had the perfect vantage point, so some of my friends came over, too. It was such a beautiful day."

"I remember that, too. It was a perfect fall day."

"Hoboken lost a lot of people," Terry bit his lower lip and nodded. "I didn't know any of them personally, but there are a lot of names on that memorial on the pier."

"I wasn't far from you that day. I was on my way to work, sitting in a bus that was stopped halfway down the helix, waiting to go through the Lincoln Tunnel. We were stopped for a few minutes and I looked out the window and saw smoke coming from The World Trade Center. It was a lot of smoke, right at the top of the tower, so I thought maybe a plane had crashed into it, maybe one of the helicopters that flew in and out of that area every hour of every day. An interior fire would not have given off so much smoke, I didn't think."

"Maybe it could be an explosion, but how would somebody plant a bomb that high? The guy next to me had a portable radio and he started telling everybody what was happening. 'It's a plane!' We could see the second building get hit. I was so transfixed by this peculiar event that I didn't yet associate the fact that my daughter's New School dormitory was two blocks away. Then we saw the buildings collapse, but I couldn't bring myself to believe it was on purpose. I was astonished, but didn't think she would be affected."

"Did you finally go through the tunnel?"

"Yup. We were the first bus through. The bus driver was a Black woman who was tough as nails; she could easily have freaked out, but she didn't. I was scared though. I thought we might get blown up."

"There was a movie about a bombing in the tunnel."

"Guarantee I'm not going to try to see that one. I still have nightmares about Psycho and I saw that in 1961. When we got to the bus terminal in the city, the driver said everyone could stay on the bus and go back to Montclair, but by then, I was getting worried about my daughter. I felt like you. I wanted to do something to help, but going down there to try to help her would just complicate matters. It'd be blocked off, and she'd probably be evacuated somewhere. I didn't get through to her by cellphone until I got to my office, and I spent all day sitting at my desk waiting for news."

"The lawyers were going in and out of offices 'increasing their ignorance,' as my father would have said. One intoned gravely, 'This is an act of war.' He aimed his remark at my boss but I butted in. 'Against whom?' He gave me a dirty look and went on about mobilizing the military and whatnot.

"In the end, my daughter and her dorm mates were stuck inside until the electricity went out and then they had to walk uptown in ash that was sometimes up to their knees. They knew some of it was human. Horrible."

It was like telling ghost stories around a campfire, mining Hurricane Sandy for emotion but knowing there was no present danger to us.

The wind of this hurricane came from the east and crashed into our windows, but they weren't rattling, so I wasn't too worried. I put my computer underneath my desk and gathered my passport and other papers and put them in a big purse. We made plans to escape to the bedroom or maybe even the bathroom if necessary, but it was all on the level of superficial talk.

We were never scared.

As night fell, parts of Manhattan turned from a sparkling tableau to stark, blacked-out silhouettes, and we expected we'd lose electricity soon, too. Meanwhile, we went into Terry's office to watch television.

By morning, it was quiet outside, and our lights didn't work. We were grateful to have a gas stove to cook on and a landline to make phone calls, though nobody we called knew much more than we did. There was no newspaper at our door, no cellphone, radio, television, or computer.

I wasn't afraid of what might happen in our lives because of the hurricane. I'd been the breadwinner in my two former marriages, and now I had a husband who could support me, if needed. Terry was on track to make $120,000 that year, of which under $17,000 would be spent on housing. I owned my car outright. My children were teetering toward self-sufficiency. We had investments and I was getting my late first husband Ernest's meager social security. We could withstand some losses, if that's what was happening.

For the next two days, we rose with the sun and went to sleep when it set with no idea what had happened outside the observable world. We were living in a world of long ago when news traveled slowly.

I wasn't pleased when I learned that our toilet flushed with the help of an electric pump that brought water up to the top of the building. I'd been expecting we could use the water from the bathtub to flush the toilet, but the mechanism did not allow for that. A generator kept one of the three elevators running so we could get to the toilets in the basement, where gravity kept the water running. On the third day, I washed my hair in the basement laundry room sink.

Centuries ago, only kings and queens caroused past sunset; everybody else went to sleep. I grew up before television—I saw my first *Howdy Doody* when I was about seven—and tried to remember what we did in the evening before we could watch baseball games and TV shows. I pictured my mother knitting and my father reading in the armchair in the living room. I think I played the radio a lot…but now we didn't even have radio connection. People two centuries ago had read books by candlelight, but I found it difficult to do. Abraham Lincoln must have been highly motivated.

Terry and I played gin rummy. I was curious why he didn't take out the GO board, but being beaten by him at cards was just as much fun. I am not competitive and the location of, say, the five of clubs is doesn't interest me. I made an effort because I didn't want to be a dull partner, but faced with Terry, a numbers whiz who could remember where the five of clubs was, I didn't expect to win unless I hit a lucky streak, which happened occasionally.

The candlelight was dim and flickering so I had to look closely at the cards to be sure I was reading them correctly and that became tiresome. I went to bed as soon as I felt a twinge of sleepiness. Terry was a night owl, and stayed up reading. He placed several candles on the table so he could see. Terry was more highly motivated than I.

We wanted to use the elevator as little as possible because if the building's generator ran out of fuel and it wasn't running anymore, we'd have to walk down 18 floors to the basement, then 18 floors back up, to go to the bathroom. If it went on long enough, we could set up some kind of chamber pot, but how would a person do that? Would we dump the contents off the 18th floor balcony, the way they did in Romeo and Juliet's time, fouling the streets below?

By the time it hit the ground, it would have spread through the air and would join the contents of everybody else's chamber pot splashed around the neighborhood. In Romeo and Juliet's time nobody lived on the 18th floor.

The alternative would be carrying a heavy, smelly chamber pot down eighteen flights of stairs.

Even if I'd lived on the ground floor, I wouldn't take to the bucolic diversions enjoyed by Walt Whitman or William Wordsworth strolling along the riverside, melding with the flowers. I felt spoiled. Lots of people in the world live without electricity, and in theory I didn't feel I was any better than they were, but this was a practical test of my theoretical egalitarianism.

Electricity was very hard to give up.

Chapter 17
Escape to the Country

Our oblivion was savory at first, an existential challenge, but four days in, we were getting restless for news. What was happening elsewhere? Were the trains running? The buses? Could we get gas for the car? How severe had the damage been? Terry was prepared to wait it out, but I was uneasy and called my brother John to see if we could come up to Vermont and stay with them until things got sorted out around New York.

We had half a tank of gas, enough to get us partway to Vermont under ordinary conditions, but the two roads out of Hoboken were choked, and we inched along, with the engine running all the time.

Once past the chokepoint, we sailed north on empty roads. For the first time in days, we had access to the news on the car radio. We hadn't seen any flooding in Hoboken, but on the west side, it was "like a bathtub," the mayor said.

In New York, there had been deaths, the subways weren't running, it was a catastrophe. The news reported that gas stations had run out of gas and I obsessed over the needle leaning farther and farther toward empty as we passed one closed gas station after another.

"There'll be gas after we get farther north," Terry said.

"What if everybody else thought that and they've all gone up there and taken all the gas?" I said.

"We'll be fine," he said. He turned away from the road for a second to look at me. "You're behaving as if your close attention might serve to fill up the tank."

"I don't want to have to abandon the car and walk back to Hoboken?"

"We'll be okay."

"Is that based on information or on the law of probabilities?" I asked.

He laughed. "You'll see."

I had no choice, so I tried to settle down, and half an hour into our trip, we found an open gas station. It was such a relief to see the needle settle at 'Full'.

In Vermont, they were not so impressed with our hurricane stories, having suffered Hurricane Irene the previous year when whole houses were washed away down roiling rivers and long sections of highways collapsed when their supporting earth washed away.

Terry was casual about New York's prospects for recovery. "We'll find a way to come back. We always do."

"You New Yorkers! You talk as if the place was magic."

"I believe we've been through worse."

I was not convinced. Hurricanes were becoming fiercer. Supply lines had faltered with Sandy. Infrastructure neglected for years, such as the subway system, came close to failure. The New York government didn't seem prepared.

I relaxed at my brother's house. My other brother and his wife joined us for chatty dinners and I played piano duets with my sister-in-law. Terry showed me the places where he'd lived when he was in his 20s. We visited his oldest friend Peter G. (not the professor Peter B.), who had come to Vermont when Terry did, and stayed.

Hurricane Sandy had not affected Vermont, but even if the electricity went out, the wood stove would warm my brother's house, and, best of all, we could walk freely out the door without taking an elevator. I felt comforted that the sources of food were also nearby; we didn't have to worry about shipping it by truck from god knows where.

"We should have a house in the country," I told Terry.

He shrugged. "We already have a home in the country and we never go there."

Terry's last years with Hugo were chaotic and he needed a place to get away, so he bought a house on the Delaware River in New Jersey an hour and a half away from Hoboken—the perfect 'house in the country'.

By the time we met, the house had flooded three times in five years, and Terry had redesigned and re-built it all three times, putting all the electricals on the upper floor.

"During the second flood," he said, "I stood on the hill behind the house and watched the flood carry away tall trees like toothpicks. The water swirled up the riverbank—that's more than 20 feet—ripping away everything in its path. You can't believe the power of a flood until you see it."

The first flood was a once-in-a-century flood, and the other two were once-in-fifty-year floods. Playing the odds that three catastrophic floods would be it for a while, he threw himself into the final renovation, removing the upstairs ceiling to expose the rafters, giving an airy, open feel, with the fireplace at one end of the main room, the kitchen at the other. Sitting at the dining table we looked westward over the wide Delaware River, especially gorgeous at sunset. We overlooked the Hudson River in Hoboken and the Delaware River at the country house.

Tranquility, beauty, and relative proximity to Hoboken recommended the house, but I didn't feel comfortable there. There were wasp nests on the upstairs deck, and with no screen door into the kitchen, there was a parade of stinging insects so constant that I stopped using the upper deck. We had to call the exterminator to eliminate carpenter bees. Insects love rivers and humidity and they adored the Delaware River.

The downstairs was dark and cramped, the bedclothes were dark brown, the bathtub had a crack with sharp edges so brutal that I only took showers. There were side by side bathrooms, with the glass walled shower as the barrier between them, meaning I might walk in on somebody taking a shower or somebody might walk in on me. When nothing was done to remedy the problems, I turned against the house.

Besides my objections, our schedules worked against visits. Either Terry or I had a class five, sometimes six, days a week during most of the year, and I often sang with the choir on Sundays. Quickie Saturday visits were more stress than pleasure.

To Terry, the river house now represented repeated trauma and dashed hopes, and I didn't want to cause him pain. He paid the taxes on the house and made no move to sell it. On the occasional beautiful day, we drove out into the country to visit the nearby vegetable stand and check up on the house.

Terry's phone beeped occasional alerts from the Delaware River Authority, and every time rain was forecast, he followed the radar reports. If there was another flood, there was little we could do. We were in a state of constant alert. This house was not a refuge, it was a sore point.

My amateur psychoanalysis was that the house on the river fell into the kind of outcast category that garnered Terry's sympathies, like the brilliant men and women who sat in a corner unused despite their obvious brilliance. The house had great promise but under the pressures of daily life, it had fallen apart. It was nerve-wracking to keep it, but painful to divest.

We stayed in Vermont for five days, then returned to find our building unaffected, but the places where we shopped and ate were. I was worried and made my case to Terry. "If there's another disastrous hurricane, or if somebody carries in a nuclear bomb in a suitcase, which they say could happen, we'll be a prisoner of the real estate market of the moment. We'll have lost the opportunity to choose where we want to live. I really liked Vermont, but not necessarily Vermont, it could be another place far enough away from New York to grow some vegetables and if necessary a chicken. We could keep the Hoboken apartment, but it would be nice to have a house in the country."

Terry said, "Let's start looking."

We took day trips up the Hudson River Valley and into the Catskills to look at properties.

I liked Cold Spring, but one look at the house prices disabused me.

Terry got nervous when other people drove, me included. He drove for hours without the radio, just as he read for hours without a break. I was more easily bored than he was and insisted on music.

He connected his iPod with his playlist on it. He liked Delta Blues, and told me more than once the story about Robert Johnson, who went to the crossroads with his guitar and sold his soul to the Devil. I had a couple of anecdotes to tell him too, such as that Bonnie Raitt said that Muddy Waters was the sexiest man she'd ever known. We listened to John Lee Hooker and Howlin' Wolf, Pinetop Perkins, and Blind Lemon Jefferson. Terry was a Grateful Deadhead, and we shared a fondness for rock 'n roll, so we listened to that, too.

Tired of his playlist after a while, I got together my own playlist, which tended more toward Simon & Garfunkel, Joni Mitchell, James Taylor, the Beatles, lots of jazz piano, and some classical. I made sure to include Julian Bream and Andrés Segovia because Terry loved the guitar. He had seven guitars, acoustic and electric, and fiddled with riffs and exercises, but I never heard him play a complete song.

When we were tired and impatient to arrive somewhere, we played Jerry Lee Lewis's *Last Man Standing*. It provided the illusion of excitement even if you'd been stuffed in the seat for hours. According to the album blurb, Jerry Lee came to the studio every day in his pajamas.

Terry liked that.

Chapter 18
Lost and Found

Starting in elementary school, Terry's wide-ranging intelligence had been rewarded, and he continued to be rewarded in his teaching career. By contrast, he found his physical self-unwieldy, though I reminded him that he walked so lightly across the floor that I usually didn't hear him coming. He'd been a decent baseball pitcher and a formidable defenseman on the basketball court, a crew member on a racing yacht, he'd progressed well in tai chi, and now he could hold his own as a tennis player.

He was a valued member of Stevens's faculty despite the fact that he had not finished his doctorate, but in the summer of 2013, that caught up with him. Stevens was aiming to raise its profile and Terry, with only an M.A., was a drag on their roster. Also, the professor in charge of the program Terry taught in left Stevens for a job in Chicago.

It took him a good week to tell me "They said they wouldn't have any more classes for me."

This was a shock. "Oh no! How do you feel about that?"

He shrugged. "It doesn't much matter how I feel."

"But you were the teacher of the year just a couple of years ago. How could they do this?"

"They want heightened accreditation and need their teachers to have PhDs."

"You've been teaching this subject for forty years. That should count for something."

"It doesn't." He didn't want to talk about it, but I could see he was grieving.

"I'm really sorry this happened."

Terry made work for himself in his office. He'd had projects and interests all his life, but his identity resided in his teaching. I urged him to keep doing it. "Terry, surely there are students everywhere who could benefit from your teaching, even if you taught for free."

He looked at me for a long minute. I didn't know if he was going to answer. "I'll never make the money I made at Stevens. Look how little you make at Montclair State. It's not worth it."

"Maybe not for the money, but you can be useful to others, give something back."

He shook his head. "I had such a good deal at Stevens. I'll never find anything like that again."

He didn't stare into space all day as my second husband Tom had done when he got laid off. Terry read books, kept the budget, followed the sporting news, did the shopping, and read the New York Times. He'd need some time to reorient himself.

Her perked up when his oldest friend Peter G. invited him to come along while he went to Australia for a conference. He and Peter stayed in an ashram in Melbourne, saw kangaroos, and visited an extraordinary botanical garden near Sydney. When Peter G. went to Brisbane for his conference, Terry visited New Zealand, where he caught the third Hobbit film when it first came out in a theater with comfy sofas instead of regular seats within sight of the mountains in New Zealand where the movie was filmed.

He was in better spirits when he got home.

Chapter 19
Kudos

In 2014, my first book was published and won three awards. They weren't the National Book Award, but they were highly competitive. Over the years I was writing it, I'd brushed aside the drone of people telling me that only a minuscule number of manuscripts get published, and their patronizing commentary—"You're writing a book? Well, good for you! I might write a book someday." They spoke like a first-grade teacher patting a diligent student on the head. I felt I had proven that intention is more powerful than statistics.

When I learned about the awards, I quit my teaching job so I could write full-time. I was 72 and had to get cracking if I was going to write another book or two.

With no outside schedule, we settled into a routine that better suited our individual habits. Mine was to arise in the early morning in time to see the sun come up over the city, do an hour of yoga, have breakfast, read the paper, and get to work. Terry stayed up later than I to read or fiddle with his guitar. If I arose after first falling to sleep, I usually found him sitting in his chair reading. Book after book. His office shelves were lined with books and there were hundreds more stored in the warehouse. He often picked up one or two when we passed the used bookstore—this was one he was missing from some author's series, or a Nordic mystery from an interesting new author. Terry had read *Don Quixote* by the time he was twelve, though he never read *Winnie the Pooh* or *Alice in Wonderland*.

Though Terry was an insatiable reader, he had not read many memoirs and didn't have the academic vocabulary to evaluate my book. He rhapsodized about science fiction writers and urged me to read Ursula LeGuin. I did, but for female writers, I turned more naturally toward Virginia Wolff or Toni

Morrison. I gave him points for reading my book about escapades with other men without jealousy or anger.

The presentation ceremonies for all three awards occurred simultaneously in Chicago, and now I could plan a trip without consulting my teaching schedule.

Terry was such a bibliophile that I thought he'd be interested in this literary event, but he declined my invitation to come along. I wondered why, but he didn't explain. If he viewed my book as a vanity project, he would never tell me that truth anyway, so why ask? This was my achievement and I felt validated for all the years I'd taken to write it.

For the first time in seven years. I was the one who would have to remember the airline tickets, the credit card, bring along the key to the hotel room, hail a taxi.

On the morning of the presentation, I had a repulsive breakfast of dry Danish, watery orange juice, and syrupy coffee at my hotel, then took a taxi to the venue. My driver told me how much he admired Donald Trump. "I just like rich men," he opined. I was glad Terry wasn't along. He would not have been interested in what his taxi driver thought about Donald Trump, but I listened to his life's story. He gave me a glimpse into a way of life and a way of thinking I knew little about.

I milled around with other authors, got my picture taken, and saw some of Chicago. I started a chain of Facebook friends and pocketed business cards.

Tired of the small talk, I took my buffet baked ziti into an adjacent room with floor to ceiling windows overlooking Chicago and the lake. It was late afternoon and the clouds were forming into a meek sunset shedding orange and red over the huge lake's horizon, as distant as an ocean's. I was high above the rest of the buildings, a mini version of New York as seen from the top of the Empire State Building.

I remembered hearing famous actors say that they brought their Oscar home, put it on their mantlepiece, waited for the phone to ring, and nothing much happened. What should I do to make my awards work for me? Ideas for publicity were not flooding into my head. In order to be a good writer, I needed to reflect and pace myself, to respond to inner story prompts, not products or customers.

I was so delighted to have accomplished one of my goals in life that I didn't care about the number of copies my book sold. I enjoyed the bookstore readings, the workshops and radio interviews, but my interest was literary, not pecuniary. It wasn't that I expected to make a lot of money on a book, I never thought about it.

If I wanted to be recognized as an author, I would have to write more books, and that's what I planned to do.

Being solidly married conferred an old-fashioned confidence, even if I was traveling alone. I'd had two wedding rings on my finger before, but neither time did my husband keep his part of the bargain. Now I was a settled member of the wives' club, a member of the gang. I felt the difference as I chatted with a room full of strangers.

There were few adult moments when I'd lived without despair or lurking anxiety. Items had to be prioritized: car repairs, taxes, a musical instrument for my talented child, new winter boots, vacation, piano lessons, the dentist. Now I had not only a comfy cash cushion, I also had affection, support, and love surrounding me. Sooner or later something would rise up and try to knock me off my pins, but now was my moment to luxuriate.

In Chicago, my greatest worry was whether I could find a cab back to my hotel.

The value of bringing along a spouse to the awards ceremonies proved equivalent to bringing a spouse to the class reunion. The spouse stands back and watches their beloved receive honors, kisses, and congratulations, but agrees to be forgettable. Terry didn't miss much.

Chapter 20
Taking Care of Business

In Montclair, then in Hoboken, we'd scrambled along with the housekeeping and compared to the rest of the world, we weren't doing so badly. The generality for men of my age was that they had not been raised to do housework and they had a lot of catching up to do. I realized that although I knew how to iron a shirt, for example, this common chore was a challenge to people who had never ironed a shirt, or made a pie crust, or scrambled an egg. A few renegade women friends in my generation preferred living in filth to doing housework, but I valued cleanliness and tidiness.

I had previously tried to redistribute my default housework assignments by either coming to a job-sharing agreement, putting my foot down, or complaining, but somehow, I always got left with the bulk of the housework. I tried going on strike, but that was equivalent to agreeing to live in filth because nobody else in the household cared if the bathroom was never cleaned and we ate pizza every night. I was astounded how long members of my household could stack dishes in the sink, next to the sink, on the counters, before putting them in the dishwasher.

Here I was, an educated, hard-working person, overcome by dust bunnies and overflowing garbage bags. The self-satisfaction of my mates (including the two husbands before Terry) over their accomplishment when they completed their assigned chores just made things worse. I'd already extracted more from them than they had planned to give. They weren't used to thinking about dishes, garbage, and the leftovers in the frig. They didn't even notice.

My father's cooking skills stretched to preparing his morning coffee and my older brother John prepared rudimentary dishes when needed. My mother had been raised in a household with a cook who had every Sunday evening off, leaving my mother and grandmother in the kitchen to cook one meal a week.

My mother remembered her mother's directions about cooking peas—they were mushy and tasteless. Having to take care of the house was a big change for my mother when she married. I didn't want to be a 'lady' the way my grandmother was, where all the household chores were done by others, but I wanted an equitable distribution of both mental attention and physical work when it came to running the household. I didn't want to have to *ask* someone to take out the overflowing garbage bag, didn't want to have to *explain* why whites and darks should be either washed in cold water or separately.

By the time Terry and I set up together, many household chores weren't done anymore—ironing was extinct and machines did some of the chopping and dicing. I had high hopes for Terry. He'd lived on his own for many years and was a good shopper and cook and did the laundry okay. He had a higher tolerance for wrinkly clothes than I did, but if he was going to do the work, he could do it his way.

The situation was better than average, but slowly, I became resentful, irritated, because of all the little tasks, outside the more general assignments, that I had to do if I wanted to live in an orderly house. I flashed back to the state of the apartment when I'd first seen it. Terry claimed to be ashamed and uneasy living in such disorder, but he had tolerated it for a long time.

Falling back into the pattern of general housekeeper, especially after my hopes had been so high, was deeply disagreeable to me and we had a few snippy exchanges about vacuuming, dusting, garbage removal, cleaning out the refrigerator, window washing, and various other chores that were falling by default to me.

Instead of remonstrating with me, Terry acknowledged the unfairly apportioned ratios of housework and suggested we hire a housekeeper.

Rocio was a youngish woman from Colombia who spoke no English. This would be an opportunity for me to speak Spanish as well as getting the housework done!

But I still had to think about the housework. Before Rocio came, I had to be sure I told her to clean the top of the stove or vacuum under the bed, and so on. I also needed to know how to say "coat hanger," "oven racks," "dust bunny," "whisk broom," and many more words that hadn't come up when I was studying Spanish in the university. I either had to twist the language into something that would express my wish, or look it up in the dictionary. I was always cordial and I think she liked working for me because I paid her $20 an hour (nobody works for me for less), and I sort of spoke Spanish.

Rocio worked by rote, and there was always a lot of work left for me. "She does the minimum," I told Terry, "but not the extra things. I'd rather do it myself." Here I was, complaining about the housework again. Nagging. Irritated.

"You're not going to like that," Terry said.

"But I have to think about it anyway. Sometimes it's not so much the time or the labor, it's having to think about it all the time."

Terry then amazed me.

"I'll pay you what we're paying Rocio, two hundred and forty dollars a month." What a splendid idea! My resentment disappeared.

Chapter 21
Finding Paradise

Besides adjusting our housekeeping, we adjusted our travel plans. Terry wanted to extend our visits to my son in California to include a place called Sea Ranch. During a teaching stint at the University of Redlands in California many years before, he had traveled up and down the state and was enchanted by that community, four hours north of San Francisco, built on a former sheep ranch that stretched along ten miles of Pacific cliffs. It had been planned by prominent architects as a grand experiment in architectural design and ecological stewardship. I resisted at first because it felt like he was inviting me to a museum, but agreed to go along.

We drove up Route 1, a storied highway that winds its way along the ocean, sometimes only steps from a steep drop-off to massive rocks and pounding waves hundreds of feet below. The driver's eyes cannot leave the road for a minute; a truck might be coming around the bend, a rock might have fallen into the road, there are cows sometimes.

We settled into our rental house and within a day, I was enchanted, too. I walked for hours either along the cliff walking path, where the ocean birds flew at eye level, or on the roads around the many wide meadows where bleating sheep were grazing, where bobcats and foxes lived, above which hawks circled all day.

One day there was a bold sign along the road "MOUNTAIN LION SIGHTED. BE CAREFUL." Sometimes, I crossed Route One and walked up the mountain to the little café across from the airport.

The air was crystalline, having been freshened by crossing the ocean, there was no traffic. At the Saturday farmers market I bought Manzanita Blossom jam from a woman in a crocheted hat wearing a lumberjack's shirt. She told me the natives of the region used the Manzanita bark to tame Poison Oak, ate the blossoms, and used the wood as firewood. A rangy farmer introduced me to his New Zealand Spinach and buckwheat sprouts.

We had a hot tub on the deck and in the late afternoon I relaxed in it, sometimes with Terry, watching darkness fold into the meadow and the stars come out in a splendor I had witnessed only in Hawaii. We also viewed stunning sunsets from the Hoboken apartment, but sitting in a warm hot tub looking out over the meadow was better.

During the day, hummingbirds visited as I sat reading outside. I became sensitized to their buzz, a touch louder than bees. They traveled in pairs and arrived at the same time every day, darting in and out of the blossoms in the garden. The California Bluebird flew back and forth across the meadow on a repeating errand.

My family is full of bird watchers who travel with binoculars. I didn't have the patience. There was a Red-Eyed Vireo up in that tree or a wren in that bush, but I could not find it. I could see the large osprey on its nest, bare against the sky at the top of a tall evergreen, and herons swooping low over a swamp, but had never seen a hummingbird up close. At Sea Ranch, the birds lived their daily lives close enough to see their coloring and track their habits.

Terry spent hours finding the iconic homes on Sea Ranch, some cleverly designed to capture the forest experience of the mountainside on the other side of Route One, others were sited next to the meadows near the sea. On my walks, I could see into the studio of an artist, his paintings stacked against the wall, light flooding through a skylight.

The homes were often built of experimental materials, and all complied with the Sea Ranch rules. There are no fences to contain the many meadows, all nighttime lights point downward so as not to invade the darkness. Roofs slope to blunt the winds coming off the ocean, houses cannot be more than 24 feet high and must blend into the surrounding terrain, some are built into hillsides or partly underground.

I often joined Terry on his architectural road trips around Sea Ranch, and we talked with realtors about available properties or lots. We stopped to appreciate beautiful views, a path beneath overarching trees, the freshly baked morning Danish at the café, wild whitecaps that traveled to shore and crashed noisily on the rocks, the seals sunning themselves on the beach. I wanted this beauty to take over his brain, to replace the sadness. He was still grieving the loss of his career, his status, his connections, but at least he didn't seem to be sinking anymore. The healing would take time.

We measured lots and in the empty space discussed floor plans—which room would have the full view of the ocean? Would there be a fence around the small area around the imagined house where fences would be permitted? How would the sea wind hit the house? Should the porch be in the front with the view or in the back out of the wind? What trees would we plant? Did we want a garden? Where would the hot tub be? I treated these reveries as I treated his dreams of establishing a foundation—I respected them, hoped they would come true, but invested little of my own fantasy time in them.

I was comfortable in the social atmosphere of Sea Ranch. Many wealthy and famous people rented or owned homes there, but in the supermarket, we were all treated the same, greeted each other the same on daily walks.

Terry's gnawing discomfort about his weight disappeared on the tennis courts of Sea Ranch, where he spent hours every day, playing against the ball machine if no partner was available. Terry's tennis partners were a ceramicist, the owner of a local construction company, a crotchety retired engineer, and a nice man about whom we knew nothing outside of his tennis habits. He could have been a billionaire, or a bum.

The more tennis Terry played, the better he felt, the less he weighed, the less focused on food, the more fun he had.

Walking to the tennis court, Terry carried the heavy backpack with the rackets and balls in it, and I paid attention to the wildflowers growing close to the ground or grazing my shoulder. Once we had to stop to allow a mama skunk and her four tiny baby skunks to cross the path.

We played non-competitive tennis. I was keen on placing the ball properly and keeping long rallies going, but we didn't keep score.

I enjoyed looking into other people's houses, checking how they parked their cars, lit their breezeways, placed their hot tub, what curtains they used, what artwork they had on the wall. My interest was not architectural like Terry's, I liked observing how other people lived.

There were three tennis courts: one looked out on a meadow with the ocean beyond it, the other was small, twinned with a swimming pool, and the third was set in a stand of trees that broke the bluster if the wind was too strong. Days were sunny, with an unfailing ocean breeze to keep us cool.

Swimming was my sport and I swam 20 or 30 pool laps every day. I was a water-loving Pisces to Terry's Scorpio.

Our vacations at Sea Ranch fell during the basketball playoffs and we ate our dinner and watched the games in the bar in the lodge. In those years, the Golden State Warriors were always in contention and we rooted for them. For one game against Cleveland, there was a room full of Warrior fans and a lone Cleveland fan. We joked with him and allowed that LeBron James was a pretty good player.

Terry's interest in sports was physical, but also historical and mathematical/statistical. His fealty to the New York Rangers, the Giants, the Knickerbockers, and the Mets wound back to his earliest childhood. When I turned away from football because of the bodies being hauled off the field game after game, he said, "I know the Giants suck, but I've been following them since I was eight years old. I can't give up on them now."

One year we came to Sea Ranch in January, hoping to see a monster storm roll in over the Pacific Ocean (None came). Terry hinted that he'd be willing to spend most of our time at Sea Ranch, as long as we could keep the Hoboken apartment and its access to New York.

The time we could spend away from Hoboken was still limited, for me, because I sang with two choirs and was the advocate for my ailing aunt Jean, my mother's never-married sister, in her assisted living facility. I visited her a couple of times a week, and when we were at Sea Ranch or in Europe, I kept in touch by phone. She'd been good to me, and I was committed to watching over her.

I hoped I would never have to choose between caring for my aunt and spending more time at Sea Ranch, where Terry was healthy and happy.

Chapter 22
There's Married and There's Married

With our changes in schedule, our accommodation to each other changed. We still had a nightly date, but it wasn't quite so special since we spent so much other time together. He worked in his office, I in my corner—but I knew he was there, heard him get up for another cup of coffee or talking on the phone, and he was aware of everything I was doing, too.

The space in which we lived our lives narrowed to just the apartment, unless we were traveling. Terry was an avid reader, just the person to be supportive of a writer, and I turned more frequently to him for his opinion on my writing.

We worked together very well in the beginning, but he had fixed ideas about the writing process. He insisted that until I got the first chapter, even the first sentence, correct, I wouldn't be able to write the book properly, and he provided copious examples of famous authors who agreed with him. We worked for a couple of months on just the first pages, but I was itching to move on.

I insisted that until I wrote out at least the first draft of the book, I wouldn't know what it was about. Sometimes taking the final paragraph of a story and sticking it at the beginning was transformative, and I wanted to get to the last paragraph to see the first paragraph in context. He wanted me to write an outline first, but after making an outline, I found myself miles and miles away from it as I sat down to write. It took a lot of work to create an outline, and what good was it if you kept ignoring it?

He had excellent suggestions based on having read hundreds, maybe thousands, more books than I had, but forcing me to focus only on the opening cramped my thinking and set me back. I was still a novice writer and my style of working was just developing. Maybe he was right. Maybe all major writers refuse to proceed until their first pages are solid. I doubted that, but then again, I doubted myself. Having involved him in the first place, it would be an obvious snub if I withheld my work. I asked for some time to work on my own for a while to see where I was headed, and of course he offered no objection, though I knew he thought I was doing the wrong thing. How many times had I heard that mixing professional and personal lives was another kind of mistake!

The problem was exacerbated by the fact that he wasn't doing much himself. Reading my work and thinking about it had given him purpose. I am not a competitive person, but I didn't want competition from him regarding my writing. He liked different books than I did, and had never immersed himself in the craft, so there was a lot he couldn't know.

If I'd been writing science fiction or mysteries, he might have been a fount of information, book recommendations, and so on, but I was writing memoir and that is a genre unto itself. In writing science fiction, a newly created world had to be clear from the get-go, and in a mystery, the dilemma had to be central to the story from the beginning. Was I wrong in thinking that memoirists have less exigent guidelines? It seemed to me that the voice was the first thing to be established.

Being around each other all day and night created the need for some space, and I took daily walks along the riverside promenade, then up the hill, back through the Stevens campus and home. Sometimes I walked west down the streets lined with Hoboken's businesses and climbed up the metal outdoor stairway to Jersey City Heights, walked north to the public elevator that ferried people from the top of the cliff to the Hoboken light rail station, and walked home through other streets with other businesses. I'd been living in Hoboken for several years but all my activities had been elsewhere. I liked getting to know the place.

As a former faculty member, Terry did not believe he would be able to access the tennis courts any more, though he never went over there to find out. He spent hours on the household accounts and taxes, followed the sporting news, read the New York Times, and books.

Sometimes he spent a day or two, or a week, 'getting organized', but his office was still a depository for books, papers, boxes of light fixtures that might or might not someday be installed, extra tennis shoes, family photos, his vinyl collection, *objets d'art* that he enjoyed but didn't fit anywhere else in the apartment. A wire sculpture fashioned by Hugo sat on his windowsill, a reminder of the talent that had gone to waste.

I could have nagged him about going for a walk or to the gym, but nagging does not become any relationship. This was his problem.

Chapter 23
Literary Adventures

Bookstore readings, radio interviews, writing workshops, conferences, and other book promotion activities occupied me. I met many people at that time, none more interesting than Joan Price. We met at a Greenwich Village store that sold sex toys where she was giving a talk about her Book *Better than I Ever Expected: Straight Talk About Sex After Sixty*. My book was about dating after 60, so we had lots to talk about, and we became friends. We appeared together on two panels at the Tucson Festival of Books that winter. In those few days, I met Sandra Day O'Connor's brother, who'd written a book about horses, Amy Tan, western cowboy writers, romance writers, and agents. I noticed that writers with a series of books, whether mysteries, cowboy stories, or romances, had lines of readers outside their booths. I reconfirmed that the best promotion for my first book would be writing another one.

Terry didn't come with me to Tucson, which left me free to think about my career as a writer without his input. I noticed that my writing was pulling us apart, but maybe that was a good idea. We had shared every part of our lives for so long, it might freshen things up.

A few months later, Joan Price emailed me saying that Eldr Magazine was looking for someone to be on the cover of their 'Sex over 60' issue, they were having trouble finding a model in New York, would I be interested? I told her "sure."

I put down the phone laughing. Me a sexy cover girl? I was sixty-four years old. I was in good shape but still…I went into Terry's office.

"You won't believe what just happened."

He typed in a few words to finish his thought, then turned to me smiling, "What just happened?"

"You'll never guess." I waited to see if he'd try to guess.

"Put me out of my misery."

"Joan Price just called to ask if I'd be a model for the cover of the Eldr Magazine issue about senior sex."

He didn't have a ready response.

"I told them I'd think about it, but I don't want to display my half-naked self to the world without your permission."

He smiled. "How do you feel about it? Do you have any qualms?"

"Not really. Fuck 'em."

He laughed. "It's entirely up to you. I have no objections. As long as they're respectful."

"Joan says that Eldr's a serious outfit."

"Well do it then." He seemed truly unfazed.

"There's one more thing."

"Uh oh."

"They're also having trouble finding the man for the photo. Would you ever consider doing such a thing?"

He leaned his head on his hand and looked at me. "Me? That would be an unorthodox choice."

"Maybe they want to show the world as it really is instead of some fairytale." This was a tricky conversation. The only time Terry was fully naked was in the shower. He seemed ashamed of his body and maybe this would be a chance to claim his size and shape, not necessarily proudly, but just as the statement of a fact that many people lived with. "They want a romantic picture, but I won't have to be naked, nothing like that. You would have some clothes on."

Terry shook his head. "I'd have to think about this for a minute. Nothing of the sort has ever entered my mind."

"It's up to you whether you'll do it. What I need to know now is whether you'll be comfortable if I do it."

"Sure. Why not?" He was treating it as if I were asking him if I could appear at a Ladies Auxiliary meeting.

"Great!"

He declined and I did the shoot with an attractive, thin, unemployed architect with bad breath. The resulting photo shows me leaning back into his arms, my skin white, his skin olive.

His legs are quite hairy.

When he saw the cover, Terry said, "That's nice."

I don't know how common or uncommon it is for a man not to be fazed by his wife appearing half naked in another man's arms on a magazine cover, but I found his reaction hilarious. Terry had his head on straight.

Chapter 24
A Darker 2016

Twenty-sixteen brought the ascendancy of Donald Trump, and Terry turned dark.

"Worse is better," he said. "If Hillary gets in it'll be more of the same and things like climate change will not get solved."

I was shocked to think that his words meant he might vote for Donald Trump. Would we become one of those families torn asunder by politics? "But your 'worse' will be horrible. There will be rebellion and war and people will get killed."

"If that's what it takes," he said.

I agreed with his assessment that radical change would be necessary if we wanted to survive as a species, but he seemed to be giving up. "How can you say that?"

We were walking along the riverside promenade to the New York ferry— not the place for an extended dialogue.

"The turning point has probably been crossed by now," he went on, "and the human race is doomed to perish of its own stupidity. There's no way we can save it."

This was more truth than I was ready to deal with. "So is lying down and dying the only alternative? Don't we have to live as if there were a future?" He was looking around at the human and vehicular traffic, but I wanted an answer. "Can you just give up?"

We had to cross a street with cars turning the corner into the crosswalk, so we had to pay attention. We reached the far sidewalk and turned to walk down the avenue when he answered. "The only way we can survive is with a massive die-out, some disease that carries many if not most of us out."

A few days before, I'd been reading about the millions of people who would be displaced by the sea level rising in Bangladesh, and that was probably correct, but I couldn't accept defeat. I never thought I'd have to defend my hope that the human race would survive.

"Well I'm not giving up. As long as there's a chance, I'm going to keep trying. Our own opinions don't matter here. Nobody knows what will really happen."

"I don't believe in miracles."

"Noah thought the world was coming to an end, too. After Hiroshima, lots of people thought nuclear war was inevitable and they wrote *On the Beach* and talked about the nuclear desert. That didn't happen." Terry's bleak worldview was challenging me. I strung together responses as we walked along. "An epidemic is all very well when it happens to other people, but I can't bear the idea of my grandchildren and their children drying from it. Giving up hope would just make catastrophe more likely."

We turned the corner toward the ferry slip and saw the buildings of the city sparkling golden in the reflected sunset.

We had no further appetite for contemplation of the end of the world—we were out for an evening of fun.

That October, the death of my beloved brother John a few weeks before the election eclipsed politics. He'd been in Arizona on a spiritual retreat and on the plane back his aorta burst, killing him so thoroughly and silently that his seatmate didn't realize he was dead until they started to disembark.

I had grappled with the theoretical, even the statistical probability that my older brother would die before I did, but the actual loss dwarfed my anticipatory sadness. He was a protective presence who had occupied a treasured space in my heart from the time we were children, but over the past couple of years, we had turned to each other more deeply during long phone conversations about regrets, our faith, and our health. We shared memories of our childhood, our parents, Christian Science. With his death, a measure of my own past disappeared.

Both raised in a Christian Science family, we branched out as adults. John embraced the ecstatic, the mystical. His eyes danced as he told me of the miracles of an Indian holy man, Sai Baba. He said that portraits of Sai Baba shed ashes.

"Actual ashes?" I was skeptical and wanted to be sure I understood.

"Right. Physical ashes. They have to keep sweeping them off the floor." He aspired to reach the point of spiritual development where his own portrait of the holy man shed ashes. He also told of a famous surgeon who had been given a stone that turned into a clock. There were miraculous healings and transmissions.

When Sai Baba was credibly accused of sexually molesting his students, John looked elsewhere for inspiration, and in Arizona, he joined a group that channeled the teachings of the great masters: Jesus, Buddha, and so on. He studied Sanskrit and brewed essential oils into potions, fashioning a custom-made one that helped me with a painful shoulder.

A photograph taken of him in Tucson the day before he died shows a man at peace.

His death pressed the shiv of mortality into my heart. John's loss was more than I could understand and more than I could express. I'd lived in cultures where there were set rituals for mourning—the 7-day sitting shiva, wearing black for a year, funerals, priests, words. In the Christian Scientist tradition there were no rituals to speak of and none of my relatives had funerals. John's wife was not a Christian Scientist, but she was disinclined to have even a memorial service. I didn't mind. A ritual would be shallow compared to the depth of my feelings.

Black wasn't dark enough.

Terry respected and cared for John, but he had not shared the experiences with him that I had, so he was a caring spectator to my loss.

My grief was compounded when my family in Vermont excluded me from the grieving process. My son had come East with his children for Thanksgiving, specifically so they could meet their Vermont family. When John died, they disinvited me, my son, and his kids, saying, "The dining room table isn't large enough."

Having been deeply influenced by many years in Europe, where the family is central, this disinvitation, especially after John's death, was unthinkable. I was angry at first, but slowly the link between me and the rest of my immediate family resumed, only a lot duller than before.

It was Terry who was my comfort and my rock. I felt proud and secure having established a family of my own that was strong enough to weather disappointment and change.

Chapter 25
Maryjane

That summer, we stayed at Sea Ranch for five weeks. I felt badly leaving my aunt alone for so long, but she had a companion who came every day and my daughter agreed to visit at least once a week. I put Terry first.

We took two trips to Mendocino, eating at the Beaujolais Café as usual. The people in the café seemed prosperous and we could tell they were locals. They greeted the café staff and each other as friends. As we were in the heart of the Green Triangle, where much of California's marijuana is grown, and has been grown for decades, we speculated about where our fellow diners' wealth had come from. People made fortunes growing pot.

Maybe I'm strait-laced when it comes to drugs because of my childhood as a Christian Scientist. In my family's house, there was a bottle of cooking sherry and some vanilla extract in the cupboard, but no other alcohol. When I left Christian Science, I began to drink from time to time, but the only time I got drunk was once when I was living in Greece.

I was horribly sick the next morning and thought. "I've done this to myself. How dumb can you get?" That was the only extreme experience I'd ever had with alcohol, and though I'd lived in Greenwich Village in the 1960s, I was a hundred percent unfamiliar with any other drugs.

Before Terry and I met, I was thinking that I ought to give pot a try at least once before I died, just to see what all the fuss was about. I asked around but one friend had exhausted her stash with her brother the previous weekend, the dealer of another friend had taken a vacation. Then I met Terry and he said he'd oblige with a joint. He warned, "It's pretty old. I haven't smoked in a long time."

Within five minutes, I had a horrible headache and felt like throwing up. "No pot for me, I guess."

"You should try it again. This isn't the usual reaction."

Terry and his friends had experimented with LSD, mushrooms, and god knows what else (no heroin), and regaled each other about their 'trips', especially the ones they took together. They loudly remembered Grateful Dead concerts.

I looked on, an outsider, appreciating how happy pot made everybody else, but accepting that this was one delight not meant for me.

In New Jersey, talk of legalization became more frequent and police were standing down, so it showed up at a couple of parties. One night, we had eight people to dinner, and afterwards one of our friends pulled out an elaborate pipe that looked like a glass dildo and passed it around. Everyone but me reminisced about the ways pot made their lives richer. After dinner, our friend Billy staggered into the living room and lay back in a lounger staring at the ceiling until it came time to go home. His wife helped him walk to the car and he headed for the driver's seat. She yanked him back. "Oh no you don't! I'm driving."

She wasn't in such great shape herself, but they only lived a straight mile away along Upper Mountain Avenue, and they survived.

I wasn't above getting tipsy with wine, but this kind of sloshed pleasure was out of my range. Terry and I never came to agree over the pleasures of drugs. I stubbornly refused to believe that marijuana had magic powers and that annoyed him.

Before 2016, when recreational marijuana was legalized without a California ID card, Terry visited the dispensary in Mendocino as if it were a museum. The clerks couldn't sell him anything, but Terry liked to chat with them anyway. Dozens of varieties were displayed: grown indoors, grown outdoors, vapes, edibles, concentrates. He engaged in speculations about methods of taking some home to New Jersey, where it wasn't legal.

In 2016, he went to the Mendocino store with an agenda. Marijuana had been legalized in California and for our five weeks in California, he could do as he wished.

"I can't get used to the idea of walking about with some pot on me without worrying about getting arrested," he said.

It wasn't much of an issue because Terry had lost much of his sense of smell and part of his sense of taste, and he attributed that to smoking too much marijuana. It was an exceptional evening when he partook, and I was relieved. The mere smell of the stuff gave me a headache.

Chapter 26
The Nurse

The first half of 2017 was spent recovering from a botched operation to repair prolapse of my pelvic organs. Until I had a reparative operation, I was in too much pain to walk or drive and largely bedridden. "You would have been a wonderful nurse," I told Terry. "You're patient, and you don't shy away from things other people might find disgusting."

He laughed. "I have been a nurse sometimes."

Terry's father John had spent his last few years in the second bedroom of the Hoboken apartment. His mother lived in an assisted living facility nearby, but the day-to-day care, in the room that was now Terry's office, fell to Terry and then-Joan. The neighbors on the 18th floor spoke well of John Stoeckert. They said that as he grew weaker, he took the only exercise he could manage, walking the length of the corridor.

Especially at the end of his own life, Terry felt regret at ignoring and underappreciating his parents, who had stuck with him through his apostasy, his Communist leanings, his hard drinking, and strange friends. After John's death, Terry took his mother to Ireland several times and was her advocate and comforter in her old age. She died of a fall following a stroke in 2003, a few months after my own mother died. What a coincidence that both mothers were born and died in the same years, 1910 and 2003.

The prayer cards passed out at his parents' funerals and a picture of a pudgy pre-teen Terry dressed up with a wide white bow around his neck for his first Communion were the only vestiges of Catholicism among Terry's belongings.

He had an inborn aversion to hurting people, unless you call ruthless games of Hearts, GO, tennis, bowling, and any other game 'hurting people'. He spoke respectfully of the most odd and unhappy residents of our apartment building, even if they had confronted or conflicted with him. Joan/Hugo had had an assortment of deranged genius friends—a brilliant composer friend had gone to jail for dealing drugs, another was an erratic, polyglot mathematician, yet another a French engineer and recherché chef whose Vietnamese wife enjoyed eating dog. Terry avoided giving the impression that he missed anything at all about his life with Joan/Hugo, but I suspect that the friends in my circle seemed tame by comparison.

He was attuned to my rhythms. If I got up in the middle of the night unable to sleep, he always shuffled sleepily into the living room where my office was. "Are you okay?" When I was sick, he assuaged my pain and nourished my body with vitamins, heat pads, teas, soups, and whatever I craved. For one stretch in my surgical recovery, the only thing, besides soup, that I could eat was the Napa Chicken Sandwich from Panera and he got me one every day, sometimes twice a day.

I didn't want someone fluttering around me all the time, and he knew when to leave me alone, too.

What a change from my first husband who told me to "get up and take a bath or something" when I was suffering a fibromyalgia attack and in pain from head to toe. Or my second husband, whose own depression blunted his response to any condition I might have.

Chapter 27
A Blow Out of Nowhere

I was amused and intrigued at Terry's attitude toward my involvement with the Unitarian Universalist congregation in Montclair. My recovery from the surgery kept me out of church for months, and nobody seemed to notice I was gone. This saddened me. I had been deluding myself that I was "part of something bigger than myself." There didn't seem to be a substantive 'something' to be part of if they didn't notice I wasn't there.

Since Terry was disinterested in becoming a member of a religious community himself, I was surprised at his insistence that I remain a member of the congregation. He pointed out the friends I had made, and my enjoyment singing in the choir.

I was offended by his analysis. "It's not just for the social life. It's because I see things in the world that need fixing, and I can't fix them by myself. You complain about the corrupted systems in this country, but just sitting in your chair complaining doesn't change anything. You need to work with other people if you want to make a change, and being a member of a church is how I do that."

When I was well enough to drive, I resumed my Sundays in church, where I was invited to take the church's leadership training course. This surprised me because besides the Music Committee, I've never been on a committee, and committees are how churches get things done. As recompense for our training, each person in the course was requested to choose an area where they could provide leadership or somehow change the congregational experience for the better.

Other than the choir, I had not found an intellectual or activist role that suited me. I felt that it was a rationalization to tell myself that I was making a substantive contribution by doing what I loved doing, singing. I had suggested some activities that would take advantage of my experience as a writer and professor of writing at the university in town, but they went nowhere.

The feminists found me distasteful, and the members of the anti-racism committee argued with me.

My ability to be the sole support of my family would not have been possible without the sacrifices of activist feminists who came before me, but there were problems in the roll-out of our broader horizons. The result of women leaving home was untended children and pizza for dinner. I'd spent several months in an apartment in Augsburg, Germany, and saw a parade of parents delivering their young children to the free child care center across the road and stood ready to agitate for a similar system in America, but that was not the focus of the feminist faction; they thought my hopes were "pie in the sky." Also, I objected to their scathing commentaries about men. I like men and don't view them as an opponent; I thought we should be working together.

Given my ineffectuality in church affairs, I entered the leadership course as an observer and found it moderately interesting. Over the winter, I tried my hand at social activism by marching to the statehouse in Trenton over issues of racial injustice. I volunteered to be a monitor, put on an orange vest, and stood at the edge of the crowd, surveilling like a Secret Service agent. The speeches were almost over when I saw a lone man with a briefcase a few feet behind the crowd. I wasn't sure how to check him out. Was he armed? Did he have a bomb in the suitcase? Was he a legislator? A passer-by? I pointed him out to the march organizers, but they paid me no mind.

That confused me, but maybe they knew who he was, or maybe he didn't, after all, have the hallmarks of a possible agitator. I was embarrassed at my hyper-diligence. I was also annoyed—why did they have monitors if not to spot trouble? I calmed down when one of the organizers who had ignored me came over and put her hand on my arm. "Union guy. He's okay." I was too damned literal, too intense to be in the business of social activism. It had too formless a momentum. I should choose an activity where I was able to contribute something others couldn't contribute, but what?

What else could I do?

I agreed whole-heartedly with the congregational goal to become a more diverse group.

'Diversity' was shorthand for Black people and gay or transgender people. They made no effort to recruit Hispanics or Asians, for example. We were overwhelmingly white homeowners too comfortable to hunger for radical change anywhere but in our minds.

I suggested that if we wanted more members coming out of the rich Black religious tradition, we'd need more than good sermons and a friendly congregation; we needed good music and home-made food.

The music was evolving nicely. With the advent of a new music director, the white folks were perking up. I was delighted when one of my Black friends told me, "When we start to sing, this place feels like the AME church where I grew up."

The Anti-Racism Committee needed a new chairperson, and they were having trouble recruiting a Black person for the job. I asked why a Black person should have to spend the time and energy needed to run a committee when racism was a white problem. Black people played a crucial role by telling us from their vantage point what entitled assholes we'd been, but the person making all the phone calls, chairing the meetings, doing the grunt work, should be white. My suggestion was greeted with blank stares.

My frustration grew, yet Terry encouraged me to stay.

In the spring of 2017, a couple was hired for the position of minister and there was a surge of new activity. The wife wanted to gather the women together on an overnight retreat. Since I'd run out of leadership ideas after the church had been nice enough to offer me the course, I thought I ought to go, though my history with retreats is as spotty as my history with committees.

The theme for the weekend was sexual harassment. We were asked to bring a favorite poem and a song to share. I chose *Wild Geese* by Mary Oliver and *Swing Low, Sweet Chariot*.

During the ten years I'd lived in Athens, Greece, from 1967–1976, I had no piano, so I took up the guitar and played and sang the songs of that era: Pete Seeger, Bob Dylan, Peter, Paul and Mary, Odetta, James Taylor, The Beatles. I was offered gigs in coffee houses in Plaka, the Greenwich Village of Athens, but I didn't want to get paid for singing—that took all the fun away. I gave a few free concerts at the school where I taught English as a Second Language and played for my friends at parties and in cafés.

I made a few feeble attempts to sing Greek folk songs and my Greek friends smiled indulgently. I had not been raised with their 7/4 or 11/7 rhythms and kept turning them into 4/4.

My New York ballet teacher, a Hungarian (where such rhythms are also common) used to complain, "The dumbest peasant in the smallest Hungarian village can dance to these rhythms!" But I had been raised hearing classical music, Jazz, Blues, and Negro Spirituals, as they were then called. This music moved in my system the way an 11/7 folk dance never would, and my favorite among them was *Swing Low, Sweet Chariot.*

In the 60s, I was surprised to be told that I shouldn't sing spirituals. "You don't have the right kind of voice for it."

"Some people might object."

Cowed by their criticism, I withdrew those songs from my repertoire. I didn't know what my own voice sounded like. Perhaps it was ridiculous, weak, unsuited. I continued singing these songs in private, but didn't play them in public anymore.

By 2017, there was a new name for what the complainers in the 1970s were referring to—cultural appropriation. I was not Odetta or Aretha Franklin, but did that mean there was no way for me to sing some of my favorite music without offense? I thought singing that music was the height of respect and admiration.

Since the retreat was billed as an opportunity to share our interests in a supportive, confidential setting, I welcomed the discussion that might ensue when I mentioned my favorite song because if we got our wish and more Black people joined the congregation we would have to decide at some point how much of the African-American liturgy and culture would be added to our own traditions. Our new music minister welcomed clapping of hands, spontaneous harmonies, and 'Halleluljahs'. The developing mix of music was garnering praise from the congregation. Did this joy and spontaneity belong to some of us and not others?

In the first meeting of our retreat, we sat at round tables, six to a table, and after the introductions there was a break. Next to me was Betsy, a fellow member of the choir, and across from me was Beverly, a middle-aged, Black woman. I always listened to what she had to say because she was wicked smart and articulate, but she jacked herself up and turned hard sometimes.

When Betsy leaned over and asked me what my favorite song was, I told her I'd wait until our minister asked everyone for their songs. Before provoking possible controversy, I wanted to see what the trend of the weekend was—I could always fall back on a more innocuous choice if I saw the current running in a contentious direction.

But Betsy teased me, "Come on, Ann, what's so secret?"

I turned my chair to face her so I could tell her without Beverly overhearing. "It's Swing Low, Sweet Chariot. When I was young, some people told me I shouldn't sing it, but then Joan Baez sang an *a cappella* version at Woodstock. It sounded sweet and clear, almost like a lullaby. It was so beautiful. So I decided to start singing it again."

When I turned back to the table, Beverly was glaring at me. I smiled at her, but her glare did not abate.

She spoke softly. "Just because it was beautiful doesn't mean it was right."

I wasn't sure I'd heard her correctly. I had been speaking so softly to Betsy that I couldn't believe that Beverly had heard our conversation. "I couldn't hear you," I said.

"Just because it was beautiful doesn't mean it was right." A hacksaw couldn't have cut through the hard edge of her voice.

I had wanted to avoid a private discussion, but here we were.

"Tell me what you think. I'd like to hear."

"I have nothing to say on the subject."

"But you seemed to suggest that it wasn't right for Joan Baez to sing it. Can we talk about this?"

She turned away. "I have nothing more to say on the subject."

The facilitator saved us by introducing Maggie, a recent college graduate with a burden on her mind. She felt that as a student representative at faculty meetings, she had not objected strenuously enough to the postponement of discussion about a rape case, and felt guilty that another young woman was raped by the same man the next week. She was in tears when she stopped speaking.

The room was moved by her pain, and there were a few minutes of silence.

"Thank you for sharing," the facilitator said. She nodded her head up and down while looking at Maggie, then she turned to the rest of us. "What do the rest of us have to say?"

Beverly raised her hand. "I have something to say." Her face was a thundercloud. "I have just had one of the most humiliating conversations in my life. Right here in this room." Her rage was boiling over.

I was alarmed.

"I won't give the details except to say that I was demeaned, made little of. You don't have any idea what it is like to be the only Black person in the room. I deal with it all the time—at work, in stores, and in church. It's not that people are mean, they skirt around it. They insinuate and snicker. They treat me as different, and I can't tell you how uncomfortable, how maddening that is."

Her excoriation of me, without naming me, felt like an extended single moment of agony. Then she paused a moment and announced in a louder voice, "I've had about enough of it. I'm done." She pushed back her chair, grabbed her notebook, and marched out of the room, the minister hustling behind her.

The facilitator was puzzled by the outburst. She looked around and said, "What was that about?"

I raised my hand. "It's about me. I said my favorite song was *Swing Low, Sweet Chariot*, and that I hadn't sung it for many years because people said I didn't have the right voice, and then I heard Joan Baez sing it at Woodstock and it was beautiful, so I gave myself permission to sing it."

Silence.

But I was just getting wound up. "You know something? The music that has come into my life from the Black community means a lot to me. It's part of my life, too. I grew up on classical music but also on Ray Charles and Muddy Waters, and Aretha Franklin, and yes, on *Swing Low, Sweet Chariot*. I love the song."

The facilitator had come prepared to discuss sexual harassment and cultural appropriation had roared into the room. She and Beverly were the only Black people in the group, so she was in a tricky place.

Beverly marched back with the minister and sat down in her seat, still a thundercloud. The minister slid into her seat at the next table, looking rattled. This incident was screwing up her careful plans to attract more Black people to the congregation.

Maggie, still emotional from her own confession, spoke out first. She didn't seem offended that discussion of her experience, which was meant to lead into a discussion of the theme for the weekend, had been derailed. "I'm so sorry to hear about your suffering, Beverly. I know white people can be very insensitive sometimes and I apologize for whatever grief you're feeling. You're such a brave woman."

A murmur of pained "Ummmm" rippled across the room.

Marilyn, a former president of the congregation, said, "We are sometimes not conscious of our positions of white privilege. It's so hidden in the patterns of our lives that we just take for granted. I cringe to think that in our church, where we care so much about racial justice, you would be treated this way."

As the women stood up one by one to vent their shame and present their apologies, Beverly glanced sideways at me. She didn't say a word, but I think she was stunned at the self-flagellation she was witnessing.

Red-haired Brenda stood up to speak. "I've never talked to anyone about this before because I never wanted to have an argument, but my husband says to me 'We're singing *slave songs? Slave songs*! It's not right! We have no right to those songs, it's as if we were perpetuating our ownership of those slaves.'" Her face reddened as she spoke.

I was in a torture chamber. These people were sacrificing me on an ill-considered altar, their sacrificial lamb. I felt like a cat splayed on its back, with wolves heading for my belly. Escaping from the room would be childish. I needed to hear this out. I drummed my fingers on the table.

The minister shot me a little smile, but did nothing to slow the onslaught.

The Chairwoman of the anti-racism committee stood up and put her hand on her chest, overcome.

"I'm just…" she stopped and bowed her head to gain control of her trembling tears. "I want to say that I'm just so honored to have been given the chairmanship of the anti-racism committee. I don't deserve it because I'm no different from all those other white people who have had the privilege of their whiteness all their lives."

She looked around the room, pulled a Kleenex out of her pocket, and blew her nose. Her voice was still wavering, but she put all she had into her next statement. "I pledge to you that I will do everything I can to end all racism, conscious or unconscious, and I know that you all will help me do that. We have a lot of work to do." She sat back down, bowed her head, put her index fingers on either side of her nose, and took a deep breath. One of her tablemates bent over to comfort her.

The facilitator announced a break and as I was leaving the room, I sidled up to the minister. "You're losing me."

She gave me a hangdog look. "Be patient, Ann. Things will get better."

I would have left the retreat at that moment, but Terry had driven me there and was coming to pick me up the next day. I couldn't call him at 9:30 in the evening and ask him to make the 90-minute drive to come get me. That would be silly. I had to be a grown up and spend the night.

The retreat center lay on thirty acres, with gardens, low dormitories, meeting and dining spaces, and pleasant walking paths. When the facilitator dismissed the group, I got out of there as fast as I could. I had no appetite for small talk with the people who had eviscerated me. I took several slow turns on a circular path. The half-moon gave a dull light, and a breeze made its way through the trees. Nature was going on her own path and didn't give a damn about what was happening to me. That was comforting.

My perspective widened as I calmed down. It was clear that I would not, for the foreseeable future, set foot again in the church. But what lesson should I carry away from this? I could not stop at the superficial observation that people I had served, sung, and donated with for twenty years were ready to throw me to the wolves. There was a deeper theological point here, one that I was not willing to represent. Contrary to some critiques, modern Unitarian-Universalism did have a theology, and one cardinal tenet was that being born white was original sin. No amount of discussion or apology, no hugs or banter could heal either what had happened all her life to Beverly, or what she had done to me that night. I could imagine a future on common ground, but that ground was a long distance from where I was that night.

Calmer and clearer, I went to my room, which I shared with the president of the congregation, a large, meek woman whose clever streak popped up at surprising times.

When she came in, she made small talk, with no mention of my humiliation. She represented the last chance to change my mind, and she seemed oblivious…or maybe she was thinking "good riddance."

Terry was due to pick me up at eleven o'clock the next morning, and he was punctual, as he always was. I flew to the shelter of his arms and we stood there for a long moment in a tight embrace. He would never betray me. He was my shield and buckler.

We drove down the Palisades Parkway, stopping for coffee along the way and on that drive, I felt a gratitude greater than ever that I had a champion, a refuge, a person who loved me. When we got home, I had a cup of tea and was checking my email when Terry came into the room and said, "Swing Low, Sweet Chariot is not a slave song. Wikipedia says it was composed by a Choctaw Indian in Oklahoma."

The irony was too blatant to be upset about. "People should choose their poison carefully," I said.

Though I retained several close friends from the congregation, I couldn't stomach any more church services, which meant I had to sacrifice the choir. That hurt.

But now, without either a teaching schedule or church obligations, the only commitment that required me to stay in Hoboken was caring for my aunt Jean.

Chapter 28
Blah at Jean-Georges

In 2017, Terry replaced the naked light bulb over the dining room table with a stylish light fixture, almost eight years after I'd first requested it. Our marriage was a slow dance of shifting priorities, and the light bulb had finally risen to first place. He found just the right one—the light aimed downward only, avoiding glare on the windows looking out on the city, and the sides were matte black, to further mute the image on the glass windows.

I was happy about the light, but wary about suggesting any other changes in the décor for fear that it would create new frustrations. We were learning all the time how to move better together.

For our tenth anniversary, December 1, 2017, he took me to Jean-Georges, one of the swankiest restaurants in New York. I was feeling giddy. "We're turning into an old married couple."

Jean-Georges is in a building Donald Trump owns or runs or something, it has gold everything, or gold-colored everything. I believe it's the restaurant where Trump took Mitt Romney to dinner so he could humiliate him by not asking him to be Secretary of State. Here was the playground of people whose values had been twisted and transformed by extreme wealth. Walking past the anti-Trump demonstrators and into the building felt a little swampy, but Jean-Georges was one of the few fine restaurants in New York where I had never eaten.

We were ushered to a nook that provided a measure of privacy. Just in front of us was a table with a single diner, a man old enough to have been rich for quite a while, in a dark suit and a silk tie, with a fresh haircut, glasses, and the manner of a pasha on his throne.

The waitress paid him visits like a hummingbird to the honeysuckle, buzzing in from the left to inquire how he was enjoying his meal, did he need anything, and wasn't it a nice evening.

She intercepted his plates so she could personally set his dinner before him with unctuous smiles.

I looked over at Terry. He'd been watching her, too. "I want her to stop sucking up to him. Come on girl! Have you no pride? He looks like the CEO of a French pharmaceutical company," I mused.

Terry twinkled me a smile. "This is a place you come maybe once or twice in a lifetime. A glimpse of the other side."

"It's disgusting."

We ordered our dinner, which arrived with squads of wait staff, each bearing a single part of the dinner—the warm plate, the sauce, the wine. Before my dessert pudding arrived, a waitress bowed before us bearing a single silver spoon on a silver tray.

I had to glance downward so as not to laugh. Terry asked her to take a photograph of us.

We checked the photo on my cellphone. We looked happy. "We're pretty lucky, you know." I took Terry's hand. "We have the means to pop in here whenever we want. The food is great, but I would prefer other restaurants with great food that are not mired in the Donald Trump cesspool."

Terry was sipping his dessert wine. I'd opted for herbal tea. "Now you're talking like me. Up with the proletariat!"

I teased him, "We do agree on some things."

"We agree on a lot." He turned to me with a loving look. "We are so fortunate." He turned pensive. "I've been thinking how happy my mother would be."

"For a good Catholic girl like her to have a Communist, atheist son was a bitter pill."

"She wanted my happiness." He looked in my eyes. "She said remarkably little about my beliefs."

I bent my head forward to lie sideways on my hand. "My mother would've liked to see me so happy, too. I'm beginning to feel like those married couples you see on television. You know, normal."

Terry picked up his wine glass again with an ironic glance. "Normal is a bit excessive, don't you think?"

"These are the golden years! No schedules, but enough money to do whatever we want. When I was young I either had enough time but not enough money or the other way around. Now I have both."

"Sometimes I wish we'd met earlier and had more time together," Terry said.

"We're lucky that we didn't have to raise children together. We don't agree about children."

"I'd be a different man if I'd had children."

"Probably. Parental ego has to take a back seat, and you learn the limits of fatigue, kind of the way men used to learn those limits in the Army. But you seem to have a children-should-be-seen-and-not-heard attitude which would have clashed with me."

Terry was amused. "You think so little of me that you don't think I would have learned as I went along?"

"Did you ever want children?"

"I suppose if Gretchen had lived, we would've had children, but when she died it took me a while to get over it and then I was older."

I gave him a gaze worthy of Nancy Reagan. "You're a wonderful person and we would probably have been fine."

He leaned over to give me a fulsome kiss on the lips, right in the middle of Jean-Georges.

By the tenth anniversary, my first two marriages were on the verge of extinction. I had never expected this turn of good fortune.

"How long do you think we have left?"

Chapter 29
Rumors and a Troll

Restless rumblings regarding our apartment building were growing. Our neighbor Angelo, a Hoboken Good Ole Boy, had breakfast every day with the pols who had ruled the city since the days when Frank Sinatra was a boy. They gossiped over breakfast at Panera every morning, and he enjoyed dangling tidbits of news.

"We're fine now," he said, "but we might not be after 2022."

"What do you mean? What's going to happen in 2022?" I asked.

"You don't know? The contract with the state ends."

The twin apartment buildings were not exactly rent controlled. They had tax abatements from the state which were renegotiated from time to time. That's what kept the rents low.

"And you think they won't renew it?" Getting information was a chore with Angelo. I had to find a way to make him feel important. "Come on, Angelo, you're the guy with your finger on the pulse. What are you hearing?"

He smiled like a fox. "We'll see. It's a few years away."

"Just the mere fact that you're mentioning this gives me hives," I said.

He smiled and turned the key to let himself into his apartment.

If the contract with the state was not renewed, our apartment could go on the open market. Terry thought we would be given a sweetheart deal to buy our own place. A two-bedroom apartment steps away from the Hudson River promenade, with a splendid view of the New York skyline, near the PATH train, the ferries, and the buses into New York would be worth a million dollars or more.

Even a sweetheart deal would be expensive. Our motley bunch of middle-class people was sitting on a goldmine, and other than possibly doing a little agitating, we were vulnerable to other people's decisions.

"How much do you think it would cost to buy this place?" Terry was a professor of Finance and Economics and over our years together, I had let the financial part of my brain atrophy.

He thought for a minute. "I don't know. There would probably be financing available."

If our money was tied up in the apartment, we wouldn't have the capital to buy something elsewhere. "If we wait until the decision is made, we won't have much room to maneuver, we'll have to accept whatever the market offers at the time."

He took it calmly. "That's not going to happen for a long time."

"We should be thinking about it though," I said.

"We'll be fine." He continued reading the newspaper.

He was right. It was too early to lose sleep over something that wouldn't happen for years, but my thinking did change one spring day in 2019. I was walking down Washington Street and stopped to chat with some young people handing out pamphlets, as I often did. I liked knowing what issues were interesting enough to push people into the streets to promote them; this time it was labor organizers.

As I picked up my shopping bags and started toward my apartment, I heard behind me, "Build the wall. Build the wall." I sensed that he was aiming his words at me, and I was unnerved.

He changed his chant to, "I'm following you. I'm right behind you."

At the first traffic light, I turned and faced him. He was a young Aryan, taller than I, blond and blue-eyed, quite good looking, well-shaped. His physical virtues did not interfere with the impression that he had just gotten out of prison. He had that anger-so-deep-you'll-never-be-able-to-stop-it look. "Are you talking to me?" I asked.

He took a startled step back, and said, "No. No. I was talking to my friend here." His friend gave him a dirty look. "Isn't that right?"

The friend mumbled, "Yeah."

There was 9/11, the Blackout of 2004, Hurricane Sandy, the threat of losing our lease, and now a political plague, with bullies harassing me in broad daylight on Washington Street.

My main prod to buy a house in the country was climate change, not politics, but the harassing conversation intensified my feelings. People talked about climate change, and we had seen the predicted manifestations of it, but few people I knew were making plans to deal with it. When I mentioned my desire to find a refuge in the country, they tolerated my discourse but did not feel the same urgency.

I didn't want to be like the woman in my (former) church who banged on the pew in front of her with both hands when she rose to bellow her concerns about feral cats, improperly sorted recycling, or another righteous cause.

Terry usually got his way, and I was usually happy to do things the way he wanted them. I could give up artichokes and beets, *The Sound of Music*, and my large office, but now I wanted something done my way, and I had to figure out how to get it without upsetting our pleasant apple cart.

I wanted to take a big step north, where water was plentiful and I could raise some of my own food and have chickens if necessary. This place could be a refuge not only for me but for my children and grandchildren. Terry's sphere of concern stretched only until his own (possibly also my) death, while mine elongated into the lives of my descendants. He loved my kids, but they weren't sewn into him. New York City, including Hoboken, would probably not become an uninhabitable wasteland within our lifetimes.

I waited for the right moment to press for a house in the country.

Chapter 30
Mistress Fong

Terry had other emergencies on his mind. He had once again lost control of his weight, and he asked if I'd consider administering the punishment with the whip. As before, this was a step too far for me, and this time it felt even farther, because his request was balanced by something transformative. I wanted a house in the country, wasn't getting it, and resisted doing as he wanted more strongly than the first time.

I wasn't sure what to do, so I called my friend Joan Price, the 'senior sexpert' of powerful intelligence and encyclopedic knowledge. How weird was this request? Was my refusal to cooperate unreasonable? She listened carefully, unsurprised that Terry had this need. She understood equally well my aversion to physically hurting someone I loved. Then I got to the point. "Do you think it would be a good idea to find a professional who could provide this service?"

"Absolutely! I don't know of anybody offhand because I don't live near New York, but I have met many of them at sex conventions, and you'd be surprised how well informed, serious, and dedicated they are to providing a service that people need, more people than you would think."

"How would I go about finding such a person?" Her words had lifted weight from my mind.

"What he needs is your permission. Let him find the person to do it."

I thanked her profusely. How many people have someone like Joan to talk to when they run up against an intimate tangle like this one?

I didn't rush to propose this to Terry. I followed my rule of thinking through major decisions for seventy-two-hours.

We were walking along the Hudson River Promenade on our way back from hearing Bill Charlap at the Mezzro jazz club when I broached the subject. He kept walking, looking at me out of the side of his eye; vigilant, wary.

"I have no objections to your finding someone to do this," I said. "There are specialists who can provide what you need."

He frowned, then he took a deep breath and looked into the distance. "Wow. Are you sure you don't mind?"

"Not only do I not mind, I'll be grateful to that person. She'll do a much better job than I do anyway. I can't be very effective at inflicting punishment when I'm crying. My whole body revolts when I have to hurt someone I love."

When we got home, he went straight to the computer to start his research and was still at it when I went to sleep.

He didn't find the right person for a couple of days, then told me he'd be going to a place called The Fortress the next night.

He was quiet the next day and I didn't try to make conversation. He took a shower, shaved, and went to stand at the door.

"How are you getting there?" I asked.

"I'm driving."

"Where is it?"

"Brooklyn."

His hand was shaking as he took the door handle. "I've told them I don't want somebody all dressed up, just ordinary street clothes. This isn't sexual, it's weight treatment. I don't want anything fancy."

When he came back, he said, "they were very nice," and showed me some red marks that would take a while to disappear. Some of them were round, not like a whip, and I wondered if maybe she'd used studs of some sort. I didn't ask. This was Terry's thing. "I told them this didn't have anything to do with sex, it was strictly about weight. She just wore blue jeans."

I was intrigued by how this world worked. There was a squad of young women—probably men, too, though I didn't ask about that—who made a pile of money as dominatrixes. Joan said they sometimes have sex with the client, but often don't. "They're pros," she said.

How many other hidden worlds were there around me?

Terry went on. "I asked her if she had other clients who were just losing weight, and she said she had a few." His mood was elevated and confident. Amazing what a little punishment can do.

I reflected again on whether I could bring myself to do what Mistress Fong had done, but I was not born to do that, or had not had the childhood experiences that primed me to do that, or did not have the brain to do that. Who knows where that drive comes from?

As it was, our sex was more like Lesbian Love. Elder Love had to be more like Lesbian Love because old penises don't rise up like young ones. Terry took Cialis, but even then, it was tame. Our sex was enough because it was latched onto plentiful affection. I never could figure out what he wanted, and seeing that it was somehow hooked onto a masochistic desire for punishment confused me more, especially since he denied that his craving for punishment had anything to do with sex.

Terry lacked the penetrative drive that most men have anyway, and I missed that, but I loved him.

I was as relieved as he was that he had found Mistress Fong, but there was a hitch. He set up an Excel spreadsheet that was linked to our electronic scale, and he would weigh himself at least once a week, on Thursdays. If he had not lost half a pound, the automatically generated number would show up in bold and if that happened, he wanted me to call Mistress Fong, make an appointment, and tell him when it was.

Once again, responsibility for his weight was loaded onto me, and I didn't like it, but it was only once a week, and until we left for Sea Ranch that summer, his single treatment worked. He lost at least a half a pound a week and didn't need Mistress Fong.

Chapter 31
Sea Ranch, Only Different

In the summer of 2019, we spent six weeks at Sea Ranch. Our fantasy of spending six months of the year there was now more possible than ever because my aunt Jean had died and left me a substantial inheritance, which changed our circumstances in some obvious and other more delicate ways. This money could make some dreams come true, but it also upset the equilibrium between me and Terry. I would have to be careful not to use my resources as a bludgeon to get my way.

Terry continued enthusing about the possibility of designing our own house on one of the few remaining plots for sale on the Sea Ranch property. All the building sites along the 10-mile length of Sea Ranch had been surveyed when the community was created in the 1960s and since then, 1800 of the plots had been sold, leaving scattered empty ones that were held by investors or were somehow less desirable.

Some were near the highway, others had a peculiar shape, or had a dull view. One plot behind a substantial sand dune intrigued us. The dune blocked the wind but also the view, so this house would have the living and dining areas on the second floor, the bedrooms on the first, behind the dune. Terry strode out the measure of our design. I rejected another plot because it was deep in the woods on the other side of Route One, where mountain lions play, and there was no sun.

These forays were an enjoyable mental exercise for me, but I was firmly against building a house from scratch. We were in our 70s, and it would take years to buy and prepare the site, design the house, get the permits from the Sea Ranch Association, find the builder, schedule the various tradesmen, furnish the inside, and create the garden. We might be 80 when it was all done, and who knew what shape we'd be in at 80.

My recent surgery had made me more aware of accessible medical care. Sea Ranch residents praised the efficiency of helicopter evacuation to the hospital in Santa Rosa and there was a well-oiled emergency response crew. But in Hoboken, the hospital was a five-minute walk away.

There had also been a spate of articles about the increased earthquake risk in California, and at Sea Ranch there was a single escape route that traversed the mountain where the San Andreas Fault lay.

When we started looking at standing houses, we learned that because of the recent wildfires, it was becoming harder and harder to get insurance. One of the fires had threatened Joan Price's home in Sonoma County, and the Tubbs Fire destroyed a neighborhood in Santa Rosa. The threat was imminent enough for us to decide to use our extra money to rent instead of buying. We made plans to rent our usual house for eight weeks in 2020.

Terry was slow moving, sensitive to my reactions, careful in his negotiations—the opposite of my tendency to impetuosity. The actions he'd wanted us to take were well researched before they were presented to me, and I usually agreed without objection once the wrinkles were smoothed out. In the end he usually got his way: the move to Hoboken, the original visit to Sea Ranch, staying in B&Bs instead of hotels, seeing plenty of Beckett plays, the design of the Hoboken apartment.

Having a pile of extra money made me cautious; it was invisible extra weight to any argument I preferred.

My own parents were a cautionary warning. My father's last words to my mother were, "Get out of here, you bitch." I was sitting next to him on his deathbed when my mother came to the door. He awakened from his comatose state and barked those words at her. It was the first time I had ever heard him say a harsh word to her, and I was stunned. They argued, but as I remember it, he did not attack her personally.

My father made a fateful decision in 1918, when he was eighteen—he left high school to join the Army. The First World War ended before he had finished Officer's Training School, but he mustered out with the cachet of an officer and began a career selling advertising space in magazines.

During the Depression, he was a captain in the Civil Conservation Corps, then he was drafted in 1939 and served until 1945. Because he was caught in the pincers of history, the core of his professional life was shredded, and he struggled financially when he returned to civilian life.

My mother came from a wealthy family who provided luxuries that my father could not provide: summer camp for the kids, vacations, the down payment on a house, furs for Mom.

He didn't live long enough after his outburst for me to ask him to talk about his anger. I have assumed that my mother's family wealth made a plaything out of his hard-won modest success as a breadwinner. Perhaps there were other factors that I don't know about, but I wasn't going to take any chances that my financial windfall would pollute the trust Terry and I had in each other.

When we looked at Sea Ranch houses, I let decisions develop in their own time. I was less enthusiastic than I had been when we started looking there before. Sea Ranch was a four-hour drive after a six-hour flight to San Francisco, and that flight felt longer and longer every time.

In our last week, we toured a four-bedroom house on the mountain side of Sea Ranch with a beautiful view of the sea. It had a high-ceilinged living room with a stone fireplace, an efficient kitchen, a master bedroom and bath, and a sunset-facing balcony running the length of the house on the entrance floor. Downstairs were three more west-facing bedrooms, two of which could be our offices. They led out onto a stone terrace and there was space for a garden. There was a large lawn, a two-car garage, and privacy hedges on either side. Terry said it felt like a 'typical suburban house' which was not a compliment.

Time was short, and Terry wanted to wait until he got home where he could figure out the finances and review the details. The $600,000 price tag was high, the fire insurance iffy.

We left for home, knowing we could come back to buy or rent any time.

Chapter 32
Light and Heavy

Our annual visit to Austria and then Dublin later that summer pushed the Sea Ranch house to the back of our minds.

In Dublin, we rented an ancient room in what several centuries ago had been student housing at Trinity College. The plumbing was cranky and there was a little side room for the servant who would have accompanied the young aristocrat who lived in this room in a long-past century.

A vicar lived above us, and we could hear him padding down the stairs as he walked to the adjacent building to take his morning shower—the plumbing was apparently upgraded only for tourists.

When we got back to Hoboken after our summer of travels, we had bills to pay, doctors' appointments to schedule, and other things to catch up on. We had tickets for an opera and a few shows, and gave some dinner parties. I was working on a new book.

This would be my first full church year with no rehearsals and no services on Sunday. I needed time to heal from the painful experience of the women's retreat. My spiritual needs were filled by morning meditation and yoga, and online workshops with the revered Buddhist teachers Pema Chodron and Thich Nhat Hahn. Their profound teachings and the meditation practice were rewarding and demanding.

Now that Terry and I were spending our days together in the apartment, we did what I'd seen many European families do when they were living in close quarters—we established routines of privacy. We still had a date every night, but during the day we spoke less than before.

When he went quiet, I didn't notice for a while. He was generally a quiet man, and the difference was slight, but marked. I asked after his happiness, and he said, "I'm fine," but his conversation felt more polite than engaged.

Then, one evening when I was just about to quickly cook and serve veal scallopine, he came to the door and said, "Hugo died."

I was concentrating on keeping the spaghettini warm until the meat was done. I thought I'd misheard him. "What?" My hands were covered in flour and breadcrumbs.

"Hugo died. Last year."

I rinsed my right hand and reached out to touch him. "I'm so sorry." I scoured his face for clues.

He stepped away.

Over dinner, he said he was walloped not only by the loss of someone with whom he had shared dramatic and life-changing events, but he was hurt that he wasn't told that Hugo was ill. "It's hard to categorize his place in my life. The closest relationship I can think of to explain it is that I thought of him like a sibling, someone I was responsible for. I guess he drew away from our mutual friends, too. I think if they'd still been in touch with him, they would have told me he was sick. He must have been so alone."

I was treading on eggshells. "From what you've told me, he'd come close to death several times. Maybe your mutual friends figured he'd come through again."

"He always escaped it," Terry's expression was studiously neutral. "He always found a way to survive, even if it meant suffering some more. He tried everything. I'm surprised that I'm surprised he's gone." He stopped for a couple of seconds then continued. "There's a terrible pathos about it. He never fit in this world. There was always the hope that this next treatment, or new apartment or friend would give him peace, but it never did."

"We haven't talked a lot about what you went through with him. It seemed like such a painful chapter. It's kind of like when John died. There were events and people that we remembered together, and then suddenly all those shared memories were gone. What you and Hugo shared was so unique that not many people would understand."

He looked down at the table and sighed. "It's hit me hard, especially since I can't even find out what happened. I saw the name of his lawyer in the obituary, and I called him, but he couldn't give out any information, just 'It was quite sudden'."

I took his hand and brought it to my lips to kiss, then lay it back down. "I'm so sorry."

He barely noticed my gesture. "You know what gets my goat?"

"What?"

"That Frances, his damn mother, outlived him. The pain she caused her children is unbearable to even think about. When Hugo transitioned, she wouldn't see him unless he came to her wearing a dress. And she outlives him! She's over a hundred now."

I made no reply because I'd already voiced my opinion about Hugo's mother more than once. If a person hurts you that badly, then tell them to stuff their money and their Metropolitan Opera gala box seats and go it on your own. I had done that with people who had abused me. Clinging to them would have made me miserable, but I had to admit that each person's experience is different. Hugo had his reasons. But this was not the time to talk about options that were no longer on the table.

Terry crossed his arms and stared out the window at the New York skyline bright and inviting on a clear night. "It's just so sad. So sad."

Over the next few days, he did a lot of staring out the window. Hugo had cared for Terry's dying father. His illnesses, his 'top' operation and gender transition, the cruelty of Hugo's mother and the indifference of his father, their plans to build a house together, the interesting, strange friends that Terry had now lost touch with, their parrots, Hugo's homemade kim chi that ripened on the balcony, and many years together. They had worn rings on their ring fingers, though they never married; instead, they exchanged vows that Terry considered solemn.

The fullness of their life together was known only to the two of them.

How lucky we were to have each other to break our falls. It's the best that true love can do.

Chapter 33
A New York Idyll

One October evening, Terry asked if I'd like to go to the Spanish food court in the newly opened Hudson Yards mall. I was tired after a busy day, but I took a nap and awoke ready to go. I put on makeup and fashioned my hair into a bun, opening both mirrored doors of the bathroom cabinet so I would see how the back of my head looked.

A chill slid from the river onto the promenade as we walked to the ferry slip. I was glad to have on my winter coat.

On the ferry, I told Terry about the local sherries and gazpachos, the tapas, the sangria, the songs I'd learned when I spent an autumn in Madrid in 1964.

Terry had lost enough weight to wear the black leather jacket that had been hanging in the closet for years. His double chin had receded to a single chin, and his tummy was a slope instead of a mound. We discussed his weight almost every day in the context of what was for dinner, clothes, budgets, or vacations. At Sea Ranch he had gotten down to 218, but was now worried that he was back up to 220. It would be seven months before he'd be able to play tennis there again and his hope to remain at 218 was fading.

His final goal was 195, but he was a tall, big-boned man. If he touched that, he'd be happy for a minute, but then regress into shame as his weight climbed back up. "You carry 220 well. You don't need to go all the way to 195. Why don't you relax? At least tonight. Relax tonight."

There was no end to his concern about his body.

In the Spanish food court, we enjoyed looking at the displays of Serrano ham, the cheeses: Garrotza, Mahón, Manchego. We shared a glass of sherry and shrimp and artichoke tapas and skewered a few piquant olives. We shared a bottle of Tempranillo with paella.

We toured the bakeries for a takeout dessert but didn't find anything appealing. Then we walked across the broad plaza to the Highline. The mall complex was spanking new, the paint fresh, the terrazzo still smooth and gleaming, the trees at most teenagers. The night was dark with barely a moon.

Hudson Yards is the northernmost terminal of the Highline, formerly an elevated railroad track that ran parallel to the Hudson River. It was now New York's hottest tourist destination. The former railroad tracks were left in place, and were now surrounded by gardens, trees, fountains, and cafes.

We held hands, put our arms on each other's shoulder and once we found ourselves alone on the dark walkway, seen only by anyone who happened to be watching from the windows of one of the apartments we were passing, embraced and ran our hands over each other's bodies, whispering I love you.

We ambled along the almost two miles of the deserted Highline to its end, then took the PATH train home. On the train I realized that this was Terry's birthday. He had taken me out to celebrate his own birthday! I'd given him a book that I called a birthday present back in August, "because you know I'll forget the day." But I usually did remember the day. October 26th.

Alert Scorpios take spaced-out Pisceses out for dinner on their own birthdays.

There was no-one in the world I would rather have walked down the Highline with other than my generous, wise, kind jester who loved finding surprises for me and revealing them with panache: Hawaii, an unexpected concert, his birthday, a lobster dinner, a special bottle of wine, a movie I'd wanted to see on Netflix.

I wanted to preserve the evening in amber. We'd each lived through the deaths of our parents and others we loved as well as national horrors: the assassinations of JFK, MLK, Vietnam, riots of the 60s, Watergate, 9/11, at least two Blackouts, various crashes and economic downturns, Hurricane Sandy. We were in our mid-70s and our personal *bon temps* couldn't *rouler* forever, but we were healthy, comfortably solvent, and together, and for those things we were eloquently and consistently grateful.

Chapter 34
Hello Vermont

When Terry suggested visiting Peter G. in Vermont, I quickly agreed. It would do Terry good to get away, and Peter was his oldest and dearest friend, not to be confused with opera-loving Stevens professor Peter B.

Besides their recent trip to Australia, Terry and Peter had shared living quarters in both Vermont and New York City in the 1960s, then Terry returned to New York to begin his teaching career, but Peter stayed in Vermont. He was the only person other than me that Terry opened up to. I hoped he'd share his mixed feelings about Hugo's death.

We settled into the comfortable house of Peter and his wife and presented a bottle of great wine as a hospitality gift. Peter surprised us by announcing he'd given up alcohol as part of his service in a yoga group that eschewed alcohol. The group also vowed not to kill, so he had become a vegetarian. Terry was a dedicated carnivore and over a vegetarian feast prepared by Peter's wife we joined in a mirthful discussion of the virtues of abstinence versus the salutary benefits of a glass of wine and a meaty lamb chop.

Given the parlous times we all were living in, it was inevitable that the conversation turned to the state of the world.

As an economist marinated in the left-wing brilliance of The New School in the 1960s, politics was keyed into Terry's general mood and attitude. When Barack Obama won the election in 2008, we were living in my house in Montclair, and we went out on the porch and yipped and hoorayed. Over the following years, the government in Washington sank into dysfunction and Trump's election in 2016 deepened Terry's customary pessimism about the future of America and the planet.

"It's already too late," Terry said. "The climate will spiral out of control, and no matter what we do, it's probably too late. The way things are, nothing's going to get done."

His acid tone was jarring and I wanted to soften it by supporting him. "It's uncanny how predictions about the climate from the 1970s are proving true."

Peter was staring at Terry. "This doesn't sound like your old ideas; you know. Impermanence, your Buddhist training."

"I'm just being realistic. Nothing we do now is going to save us."

"You spent all that time mastering meditation and—" Peter began.

Terry interrupted him with a smile. "Nobody masters meditation."

"You know what I mean. Why did you stop doing that?"

Terry shrugged. "I moved on."

"But you've moved on to a place where we're all doomed. I have to accept what the scientists are saying, but that doesn't mean that I won't continue to try to survive." Peter seemed concerned about Terry on a level deeper than mere logic.

"The only way this can be stopped is by revolution. It didn't matter whether Trump or Clinton won. Clinton would have been just as bad."

I had heard all this before, but it was new to Peter. His face turned red. "How can you say that? We wouldn't have pulled out of the Climate Accord! We would still have our allies!"

"The world is different, but they're all the same. It's the same system. There's no time to wait for things to change."

Peter's wife had been in the kitchen putting the finishing touches on the apple crisp and fixing the after-dinner tea. She was not the sort to brook talk of the apocalypse at her dinner table and she interrupted with dessert.

They spent the rest of the evening cracking lame jokes, but after Peter's wife and I had gone to bed, they talked into the night.

Terry's embrace of doom clouded our plans and darkened our relationship by taking certain subjects off the table. Why make plans if one of us thought there was going to be no future?

Peter and I were both up early the next morning and his wife had already left for work when we met for breakfast. Peter was puzzled. "What's wrong with Terry? I've never seen him like this."

I appreciated this alliance of concern. "I don't know. Maybe he's just adjusting to change. He's such a creature of habit."

Peter laughed. "In that, we are the same!"

"I hope he'll lighten up a little."

After Terry got up and had his breakfast, the two of us drove around the places where he had lived as a young man. He marveled that most of the restaurants he'd worked in 40 years ago were still there. We drove to the mountainous land he'd marked out as a surveyor. He'd served as the temporary manager of the town of Killington and showed me the ski runs there.

I asked to visit the Karma Choling Monastery where he'd studied under Chögyam Trungpa Rinpoche in the 1970s. "I'd really like to see it. You said you meditated there for four hours a day and also that you loved their breakfasts."

He was behind the wheel, making our way through the picturesque town of Winchester, where he'd also lived for a while. We were hungry and he wanted to get home and have some lunch. Because of the pandemic, all of the restaurants and cafés were closed.

"Some other day."

Cars are great places to have ticklish conversations.

"Why did you leave Buddhism?"

The sidewalks were mostly emptied, but one woman walking her dog was ambling across the street in front of us.

"After Trungpa Rinpoche died, I never found a replacement teacher." I had a lot more questions for him, but he showed no appetite for a fuller conversation.

His time at the monastery was a subject of great importance to him which he rarely mentioned. Trungpa Rinpoche was a phenomenon embodying great accomplishments and equally impressive disasters. Like the Dalai Lama and so many other Tibetan monks, Trungpa endured a harrowing escape from Tibet after the Chinese started destroying all vestiges of the ancient Tibetan religion and killing holy men.

During the last stretch of that journey through the frigid peaks of the Himalayas, his group ate their belts and leather bags to stay alive. I doubted I would have the stamina and determination to accomplish such a feat, though, of course, they had no choice and I wouldn't either.

Once in the United States, Trungpa Rinpoche founded the Vermont monastery and Naropa University in Boulder, Colorado, and wrote influential books introducing the Tibetan form of Buddhism to the West. Terry said he was an unforgettable teacher, full of surprises and insight. After my break with the Unitarian-Universalist Church, I'd taken some transformative online courses with Trungpa Rinpoche's acolyte, Pema Chödrön, and was keenly interested in knowing more about him, but let this subject lie. Terry would talk about it when he was ready.

Pema Chodron's feelings about Trungpa were as complex as Terry's. In awe of his scintillating gifts, both she and Terry struggled to square them with his egregious behavior. He womanized and drank so heavily that he died in his late forties of cirrhosis of the liver. He was the kind of 'bad boy' that Terry tolerated, even admired—someone who broke the rules, defied authority, went to extremes, and thought for himself—but he caused a lot of suffering and disappointment along the way.

Terry said he'd been spiritually reborn through his studies with Trungpa, was sorrowed and confused by his flaws, and grieved his early death.

His death ended Terry's Buddhist studies. The death of a remarkable tai chi teacher ended his tai chi studies, too. He was sure that nobody could measure up to his original mentors.

I encouraged him to look for new ones, but he didn't want to.

Chapter 35
A New Home

Forest fires in California were darkening the skies of my son's home near San Francisco, and a neighbor from Sea Ranch wrote that she and her friends joked about running down the cliff to the beach if a forest fire jumped Route One and started burning the vast meadows. She said they were confident they could grab what they needed, and it wouldn't be so bad. I thought it would be awful, but maybe she knew better.

The house we usually rented was in the meadows between Highway One and the ocean. On the other side of Highway One was the second set of meadows and more Sea Ranch houses. Halfway up the mountain the trees thickened into a forest that looked much like the forests that were being shown on television with balls of flame flying from tree to tree.

There was a fire station on Route One and another up the hill across from the airport, and a large sign on the road into Gualala had a peacock tail of warnings, from bright red to blue, a black needle indicating the severity of fire risk. When we were there, the black needle hovered around the middle, but now my friend said it was bright red.

We still planned to spend eight weeks there in the summer of 2020, but there was no more talk of buying. As a result, our house hunting in Vermont was elevated above the fantasy level.

It was fun poking into country roads, seeing houses with acreage around them that made a Hoboken apartment dweller's head spin. Terry's taste in houses wasn't always the same as mine, but we were sure we could find agreement. One house he liked had room for a garden, but only if you didn't mind climbing down a steep set of stairs to get there; it also had two floors, and a rabbit warren of a basement, all of which would be cleaned by me.

Another house he liked would need complete remodeling, which might be interesting to him but would be drudgery for me.

My requirements were: easy to clean, preferably on one floor, space for a decent garden, some sense of nature but preferably no bears in the yard. It needed enough room to allow my children and grandchildren to visit, to have people, sometimes quite a few of them, to dinner.

On our next to last day at Peter's house, I was finishing my breakfast when Terry said he was going to take a last drive around to see some houses he'd seen listed. A half hour later, he called me. "I'm coming to get you. I've found your house."

He had chosen well. It had three bedrooms (or in our proposed layout, two offices and one master bedroom), a spacious kitchen and large living room. Coming in the front door, I could see through the living room into a screened sun porch and the backyard, and looking west out the front windows, a vista stretched to the Adirondack Mountains, where my family had vacationed for 120 years.

The laundry room was off the kitchen, a major perk for me. I liked hanging my sheets and towels outside to dry, and instead of hanging them on a cramped 18th floor balcony, there was a large, sunny space off the back terrace. Tall cedar hedges to each side provided privacy from the neighbors. An unfinished dry basement ran the whole length of house under the upper rooms—we could have a huge pantry and a ping pong table down there.

My approval was instant. "It's like an apartment with a basement and a yard."

Before talking to the realtor, we clarified our agreement that if we bought the house, we would keep the apartment in Hoboken and travel there frequently. I didn't enjoy the four-hour trip, but I was open to all manner of compromise to get my house in the country.

We'd offset the extra expense of keeping both the house and apartment by cutting down on our travel budget, though we agreed that we still wanted to spend the eight weeks we'd already reserved at Sea Ranch. We'd also take our annual trip to Austria—2020 would be an expensive year. Our airline tickets were free because Terry had researched the credit cards that would give us air miles for all of our purchases. He had his father's eye for a bargain, while I am the sort of person who says, "I need brown shoes," and goes out and buys brown shoes. Terry would spend hours finding deals on brown shoes. It is possible to have a generous spirit yet be interested in finding deals.

Terry made his share of compromises in our life together, but I was more adaptable than he was. I didn't care what color the walls were or whether we had exactly the correct utensil to prepare a certain dish. All my adult life, in many different countries, I'd improvised. I'd cooked meals on a wood stove in the mountains of Zimbabwe, washed my laundry in the bathtub in Athens, Greece, learned the value of a siesta in Italy, realized how thoroughly unsuited I was to farm work on a kibbutz in Israel. But now that I had the funds to consider it, I had an implacable desire for an easy-to-care-for house with a garden.

With our upcoming acquisition I didn't feel any kind of victorious, instead, I felt more tightly bound to Terry. Waking up next to him, I thought, *Now I understand why they call spouses 'my other half'. I can't imagine being with anyone else.* We were trees whose roots had grown together, swaying in the same breeze, drinking up water from the same earth supply. Wherever I went, I felt him with me. There were some disadvantages to this closeness…thoughts I no longer thought, food I no longer ate, also sorrows I had not felt before and regrets we shared.

Just as Terry had taken on the budgeting and planning for the Hoboken apartment, I felt it was my responsibility to take on the planning and organizing in the house. It had been used as a B&B, and the owner asked if he could leave couches, televisions, rugs, a kitchen stocked with pots, pans, China, and flatware, lamps, and all manner of other things that he would otherwise have to get rid of. This was brilliant. The apartment in Hoboken could remain mostly untouched. Terry could feel easy about it.

I hoped he would recapture a version of the pleasure he had felt living in Vermont as a young man. Unlike Hoboken, there were year-round indoor tennis courts. We would still be able to travel. It would be my turn to have a big office and access to the countryside without driving along clogged and unpredictable Route 3.

We returned to Hoboken, and I began packing things I'd need to set up shop in Vermont, but Terry did little. He wanted to take care of the closing, measure the spaces in the new house, and move in March. I didn't understand his reasoning but didn't object. This was a big step for him, and he could take his time.

When we drove back for the mid-December closing, the temperature was zero.

"Welcome to Vermont," quipped the attorney.

Chapter 36
Moving In

Opening the door into a house that we now owned felt exhilarating. I walked around the property, careful of icy spots, checking every plant, though in their winter guise it was difficult to figure out what they all were, every angle of the stone walls.

Terry was restless and we spent time driving around.

I worried about the separation between the two of us that would be inevitable in a house with two wings separated by a living room and kitchen. In Hoboken, Terry kept his door open, and I was in a corner of the living room with no door, so we heard each other's phone calls and sensed each other's movements. I felt his ears upon me if I was reading my work aloud or doing vocal exercises.

We walked around and around, rearranging furniture and planning renovations. Should we have a deck in the back? Replace the stove? Build an island in the kitchen? Renovate the bathroom? Get new rugs?

When he was a professor, Terry had awed his students by doing mathematical equations on the fly but planning our future in the Vermont house revealed a dimming of his mental agility—not surprising at 76. My mental agility was slipping, too, and we commiserated when we couldn't remember the name of that Middle Eastern dish, or the actress who starred in a 1960s movie. "Maybe we're losing our minds," I said, "or maybe we just have too much in our heads. Somebody who's 30 has seen x number of movies, but we've seen x times x times x movies. There are thousands of actors and actresses to remember."

This analysis did not placate his concerns.

I wanted a carpet in the room that would be my office, and Terry called me in three times to help him take the measurements.

I stopped the frown that was forming and asked him softly, "Why do we have to measure it so many times? The room hasn't changed its shape."

He put his teeth over his bottom lip for a moment. "If we get this wrong, then we'll be left with a mess."

The rug store sent someone to measure the room, yet Terry still wanted to measure it two more times. I complained. "If the size is wrong, it will be the fault of the installer. They'll have to fix it."

"I don't think so," he said. "We have to get this right."

Terry had been trained as an engineer, but what kind of engineer would he have been, if he had to measure a room eight or nine times before he was confident of his decision? Maybe he'd turned away from engineering in the first place because of this sort of anxiety, or maybe his mental acuity was fading more than I wanted to acknowledge.

I was trying to move slowly, though there was a lot to be done. This house and its third of an acre would give security and safety to us and to my family, shielding us at least for a while from climate change and any storms or other disasters that hit New York.

The cultural delights available in Vermont's daily life lay not in fancy restaurants or star-studded Broadway productions, but in Nature. The dense trees of Vermont obscured animal behavior that the dumbest naturalist could easily track in the spare landscape of the Pacific coastline where hummingbirds had visited me at the same time every day and I could study the raven as it sat on a fencepost.

Everyone in Vermont had a dog and a garden. Terry wouldn't hear of getting a dog; he said, "Let's get a pet clam. It makes no noise and if it annoys you, you can always eat it." Having a dog in an apartment was one thing, having a dog in a house was a more welcome prospect to me, but I could live without it.

At our first dinner in our new home, we reminisced about the picnic lunch we bought in the Paris luxury store Fauchon and ate in the *Jardins de Luxembourg*. We shared memories from our many travels: the Gaudi buildings in Barcelona, the 'nose to tail' restaurant in London, glamping in Slovenia, seeing Derek Jacoby play King Lear one year, and a year later seeing Ian McKellan in the same role, visiting Terry's cousin in Frankfurt, the *Musikverein* in Vienna, water encroaching on the streets of Venice, walking through the ruins in Rome.

The memories we were making in Vermont were of a different genre; they had to do with security and control of our surroundings, natural beauty, fresh air, and silence. The street outside our Hoboken apartment was frequented by wailing police cars and fire engines, students shouted and laughed until late into the night in the park across the street, and helicopters flew down the Hudson River to landing zones in Manhattan. Here it was still and dark, and I loved it.

For the first few weeks, we took our garbage, and there was a lot of it, to the dump, then we connected with one of the local haulers. Instead of taking a few steps into the hallway outside our apartment and dropping our garbage bags down a chute, we had to lug the two huge garbage cans, one red for recycling, the blue one for general trash, to the curb.

One evening I pressed the button to open the garage door so we could take out the garbage cans, and there over the soft, sinuous silhouette of distant mountains spread a burgeoning, rosy sunset. In the near distance was our neighborhood road with quiet, well-kept houses on either side and the intricate patterns of winter branches against the blushing sky. I turned to Terry and put my arms around him, my head on his shoulder. "This is so beautiful. So beautiful."

"Yes, it is," he said, squeezing my waist.

I was worried about him and looked up into his eyes. "Are you happy, sweetheart? Are you happy we moved here?"

"Yes," he smiled "I'm happy we moved here."

Chapter 37
COVID!!!

COVID crept into our minds with whispers from faraway China beginning around the time of the house closing in December.

We were attentive to the news but didn't change how we lived.

Six weeks after the closing, mid-February, we came back to Vermont with two cars full of stuff and set about preparing for the furniture, books, equipment, and clothes that would be arriving on our moving date, March 14th. It was cold, but our new house was cozy and comfortable.

We met Peter for walks along a dirt road alongside Rutland's watershed, foaming through the rocks. At the top of the hill was a chained-off plot with the remainders of a logging operation, the round ends of abandoned logs baring the rings that cataloged their lives.

A name was given to the new virus, COVID-19. On March 1st, the first American death happened in Washington State. I bought two boxes of medical masks and plastic gloves.

We went back to Hoboken because we had tickets to see *The Lehman Trilogy* on Broadway, on March 7th.

In the audience, I listened for coughs, and avoided crowding together in the intermission. After the risk was taken, I was regretful. In the elevator going up to our apartment on the 18th floor, six people were chattering about the virus. They were skeptical. "What are we supposed to do?"

"It's probably like one of those hurricanes that is supposed to be so devastating but never comes."

"Don't you think we should at least be careful?" I ventured to ask.

They laughed. "Don't kiss me! Don't kiss me!"

The next day I was the only person in the supermarket wearing a mask. I can't say I didn't care what other people thought because I always care what other people think, but I persevered despite their curious looks. I had a tender awareness of people passing close to each other in the aisles, picking over fruit with bare hands, following each other closely through the checkout lines, passing all their purchases along the same conveyor belt.

On March 11th, I learned that the woman in the apartment across the hall had COVID. I was told to keep it a secret, which suggested that there might be other people in the building who were also keeping it a secret. There were no rules then and I worried that the whole building might be quarantined, and we'd be stuck in close quarters with virus deniers.

"We've got to get out of here right away," I tried not to make it sound like an ultimatum, but it was. "If we don't leave, we could be stuck here for a long time."

"We've only got a couple of days until the moving guys come." Terry had no sense of urgency.

"I don't want to stay here until March 14th. Nobody's wearing a mask, and we have to ride in the elevator with them. Let's pack up both cars and scram." I canceled the movers and we left for Vermont.

We took our computers, most of our clothes, shoes, and boots, a selection of books, including cookbooks, most pots and pans, and our coziest comforters, sheets, and pillows.

Our overloaded two-car caravan, with small objects in all the interstices, drove up River Road and passed under the matrix of roads leading up to the George Washington Bridge. I felt lighter when we hit the Palisades Parkway, the highway north.

In Vermont, we backed the cars into the garage to unload everything directly into the back hall, but I caught a glimpse of Terry disappearing around the side of the house with the old, red suitcase which held his women's clothes. Instead of coming in the door, he'd snuck around to enter the basement through the bulkhead, hoping I wouldn't notice.

Seeing this sent shivers through me. Why couldn't he bring himself to throw away those seedy, old-fashioned, flimsy, polka-dot blouses, medium sized heels, girdles, bras, stockings, and mid-century skirts? When my mind was forced to touch his obsession, I thought of the 'mother' in *Psycho*.

I could never admit that to Terry, but it nested in my head. I also knew that probably I should raise the subject, so it didn't turn into a cause for shame. I didn't think any less of Terry because of his affinity for women's clothes, but

I would have no sexual desire for a man wearing them. The last thing he'd said to me on the subject, years before, had been a neutral "I don't need them." Clearly, he did.

Somehow, having those clothes accessible was making it possible for him to live the rest of his life as my husband. They were thus part of my life, too, and that was what gave me the shivers. It was my fault that I couldn't accept this harmless proclivity, but it clashed with some of my own most inaccessible instincts and habits. My knees would have buckled if he'd come to me dressed as a woman. I couldn't refuse him without hurting him, but for me, it would be as if I were being forced by a stranger. I couldn't reason myself out of it.

I imagined what it would be like to be required to live my intimate private life with a woman. I had several friends who'd been unhappily married to men who turned out to be homosexual. Did those men feel the same revulsion at the idea of having sex with a woman as I felt about Terry dressed like one? Being forced to live out my sex life with a woman would be a strange kind of torture. Since Terry's male instincts were weak, I got a hint of how that would feel, though we had struck a balance where I could manage.

Perhaps if we'd seen a counselor, I could have come inch by inch to accept something that I acknowledged was harmless in itself, but Terry would not go to a counselor. Why? Maybe instead of the mid-century polyester clothes, he could wear things that were more contemporary. A lot of men in 2020 wore clothes that men would never have worn in the 1960s, including dresses and skirts, but in a different style. Though my visceral response was strong, I thought there were ways to make me comfortable with him in women's clothes. Why couldn't he at least try to be integrated in all his parts? I was angry with him and angry at myself for not being able to overcome this obstacle. Did seeing Mistress Fong overcome his desire to wear women's clothes? How did that work? Or were Mistress Fong and his cross-dressing desire unrelated? Did he have two obsessions, masochism and cross-dressing, or did one depend on the other? What dangerous mountain path wound through his soul? Could I join him in traversing it without imperiling myself?

Chapter 38
Life Without Everything

I got to work organizing our stuff, and Terry searched out the right television channels to watch the sports he loved and then, all of a sudden, there were no sports. No March Madness, no Knicks or Rangers, no pitchers and catchers. People in New York were closeted in their apartments, falling to sleep to the sound of unrelenting ambulance sirens. We would not be able to go back to Hoboken for a while. Vermont had one of the lowest infection rates in the country, and I was grateful for our lucky timing.

After dinner one evening, we walked around the living room trying to figure out how to configure it. Terry excused himself to go to the bathroom, and I leaned against the back of the long orange couch upholstered in a pleasant, velvety material. Nausea struck me so strongly that I wondered if I would be able to walk across to the sink to vomit. I took a few steps toward the kitchen calling out, "Terry!"

I made it to a chair but was too feeble to hold myself up. As Terry rushed in, I slid to the floor. I stretched my arm out, hoping to push myself up, but didn't have the strength even to move my fingers.

"What's the matter?" Terry bent down to help me up.

I thought I might be dying. I couldn't speak. This would be a good way to die. Poof!

Terry took the phone from his pocket and called 9-1-1, fetched a blanket to put over me, then paced back and forth, watching me helplessly. "Can I bring you some water? What can I do to help you?"

Shortly, I could push myself up to a sitting position. "The EMTs are going to think they came for nothing," I murmured.

Terry helped me to the couch near the front window, upholstered in the same velvety fabric, only green. I sat with my head in my hands breathing deeply as my strength returned.

The EMTs arrived, took my vitals, and pronounced me "fine."

"I'm sorry to call you out when I'm so fine," I joked.

The one named Tom jiggled my shoulder. "No. No. Don't feel that way. We're always happy to come. You never know." He packed away his blood pressure monitor and closed his black bag.

"She was so weak she couldn't move," Terry said. "It was terrifying."

The EMT smiled. "You don't have to worry. Her blood pressure's stable, heart rate good, temperature normal. Just have her see her doctor tomorrow if you can."

They watched as I stood up and walked around a bit, then bid us a jolly goodnight.

We were a five-minute drive from the hospital, another point in our new home's favor, but within half an hour, I was loading the dishwasher and wiping off the counters as if nothing had happened. I'd never had an incident this shocking and serious. I had to rest and keep an eye on myself for a few days. Terry never mentioned it again, but it had shaken him.

April arrived, the snow and ice melted, and Zoom also arrived. I signed up for qi gong classes, joined my Hoboken writing group and New Jersey Buddhist sangha every week, and used WhatsApp to speak with my daughter in Buenos Aires and with our Austrian friends.

Terry didn't take so readily to virtual living. He read books and kept up with the news on the computer. Without sports news, he felt a void.

The streets were empty; there was nowhere to go.

When we first arrived, before the lockdown, I expected that Terry would soon make friends on the tennis court, find his favorite place to go for coffee, drive around to familiarize himself with the area, and meet with Peter sometimes. We'd be traveling back to Hoboken every month or so. He'd get used to it.

That was not going to happen.

Chapter 39
A Trying Time

In the warming afternoons, we took walks in the surrounding neighborhoods, he looking at the real estate situation, I looking for ideas about how to arrange our house and yard.

Up the hill, we discovered a long road parallel to ours, and walked to the end of it, where it faded into a forest. On the way back, Terry said, "I'm gaining weight and won't be able to see Mistress Fong."

I felt a stab of fear. Was my plan to spend part of our life in Vermont going to harm Terry? I took his hand as we walked along.

"The pandemic is keeping everybody home and I'll bet lots of people are lamenting a few extra pounds."

His eyes were like a horse's when it realizes the barn is on fire. He looked from one side of the street to the other but had nothing to say, so I took another tack.

"We can drive down to Brooklyn so you can see Mistress Fong. We can go down and back in the same day or spend the night in Hoboken."

"Ann, you know that's not going to happen. If I don't lose the weight, I'm supposed to go the next day, maybe the same day. It doesn't work if I go a few days later."

I had to take a few breaths not to get irritated. "I haven't noticed that you're any heavier."

"I've gained five pounds." He looked down at the asphalt.

I scrambled for yet another gambit. "Do you want me to call Mistress Fong?"

"No. We can't go down this week. We're too busy. I don't know what to do."

Over dinner that evening, he said, "I called Mistress Fong. They're closed. Due to the pandemic, they said." I didn't like his look. He was panicking.

I placed my hand on top of his and leaned toward him. "Let's just change the rules a little, use today as the baseline and work from there. We can take walks more frequently, like the one we took today. The exercise will be good for both of us." I looked at him and smiled. "And we'll have more time together."

He shook his head. "You know what happens when the rules start to fall apart."

I was running out of new suggestions and there was a moment of stalemate, then he continued. "You know that seeing Mistress Fong doesn't have anything to do with sex, right?"

I was at a loss for words for a moment. "She's helping you preserve your sense of wellbeing and I don't give a damn whether sex is involved."

His panic surfaced again when the fuel provider came the next day. I came in at the tail end of their conversation about refilling the tank. The fuel dealer was saying, "Most of our customers don't choose such a conservative plan."

"I want to be sure we don't run out of fuel," Terry said.

"Whatever you want," the man said, shrugging his shoulders.

My feelings for Terry were swirling into a new pattern. Sometimes, when he was victim to unreasonable anxieties, my patience thinned. But turning to him in the night, I felt him as part of me, and I was grateful.

Our love was my existential state. We entered phases and rode waves together. Whatever he was going through I wanted to go through, too. He held me; I held him.

Sea Ranch was the place where he regained his optimism and joy, and I regretted that we couldn't use our reservation this year, but at that point in the pandemic, it would be unthinkable to fly to California, rent a car, and drive up to Sea Ranch. I checked the website and found that the tennis courts at Sea Ranch were closed; we'd be just as isolated there, but with even fewer resources.

If we'd been in Hoboken, I would have tried to insist that he see a doctor—I say "tried" because insisting didn't always work with Terry. Dr. DeMarco, whom he'd known for forty years, retired a month after we left Hoboken, so I couldn't call him for advice.

I called a psychologist friend in New Jersey to see if she could talk to Terry about his anxiety, his 'lostness', but she couldn't practice out of state. I didn't know any psychologists in Vermont and picking one randomly might result in finding someone who wasn't compatible, and then Terry's aversion to counseling would harden.

The move was disorienting. I was concentrating on Terry's malaise, but was also anxious myself, so I began attending Zoom meetings of the sangha at the New York Zen Center for Contemplative Care. Their spiritual calling was to attend the dying and the distressed, so they were well attuned to the exigencies of the pandemic, and I felt comforted by their thoughts and their presence. After every daily meditation, there was time for chatting, and I had someone to share my worries with, if only for a few minutes. It helped to hear the worries of other people who also were dealing with an unknown world.

The regular meditation was training my mind so that I could calm myself. It was difficult, but with persistence, I would stop myself from recycling stories of doom. The training of Thich Nhat Hanh and Pema Chodron taught me to embrace the feeling of the moment, even if it was a bad one. Instead of running away into fantasies of an even better or even worse future, I learned to assess my present, where I was safe, healthy, and comfortable. Sometimes I didn't succeed so well, but I felt I had a tool to manage my sadness and anxiety. At least a little bit.

In telling Terry about my meditation practice, he revealed a more encyclopedic knowledge of Buddhism than I had expected. He explained the history of the various branches of Buddhism, knew the original monks and holy men and women and the theology as taught by Trungpa Rinpoche. His teaching was dry, academic, and fascinating…but he didn't meditate. I thought it would do him good because it would have done him good to focus on today, when he was safe, comfortable, and well loved.

Perhaps it was good for Terry to have a companion who was not panicking as he was. But perhaps not. He had always served in the role of the steady hand when I was anxious or out of control, and I worried that switching roles would feel uncomfortable to him. He might feel he was no longer needed.

Chapter 40
Spring in Vermont

May arrived, and I pulled Terry out to the front lawn to see the daffodils, yellow heads still tightly bound in bud. "I had no idea there would be daffodils here! When do you suppose they'll open up?"

He gave a little laugh. "I'm a touch out of the loop when it comes to daffodils."

All winter I had been wondering what plants were in our yard. The guy who was doing the spring cleanup said he thought the trees were wild apples and maples. There were tiny red dots on the apple trees that I thought were budding apples, but they were the dried-up fruits from last year. I enthused over the catmint plants that were lushly opening up and learned the names of plants like hosta that lots of people have known all their lives. I looked forward to the herbs I would grow for cooking; sage, basil, oregano, chives, and rosemary.

Terry looked on as I budged out of the house, but his project was turning a closet into a pantry. He measured and discussed it with the contractor. The pandemic had made people stock up on staples and we needed someplace to put all the extra pasta, rice, tomato sauce, jams, baking supplies, nuts, and some of the lesser used equipment such as the waffle maker and the bread machine. We had extra vacuum cleaner bags, soaps, and cleaning supplies.

When the crew came to do the work, Terry stayed with them and they chatted about other possible projects. I was gratified to see him so engaged.

He felt increasingly bereft without sports to watch. The draft, the hiring of managers and coaches, the player trades, the discussion of different tactics on the hockey rink and the basketball court, even the upcoming Olympics—all these subjects had evaporated. It wasn't that he didn't have access, these discussions didn't exist.

Sports figures he'd been following for years were practicing their fast balls in their backyards or working out in their basements. He'd been looking forward to seeing how the aging Roger Federer, one of his favorite athletes, would fare in the tennis tournaments and fretted that he was losing one of his last productive years.

His favorite event was the Tour de France. It had a mix of raw athleticism and grit, but also speedy calculations and gambles—which rider should go first, when should he be spelled by his teammates, who should ride on his right, on his left, when would the riders let somebody else win a day so that they would be fresh enough to win the tour? Besides the race itself, there were controversies about doping, disputes among team members and sponsors, challenges to the leader's place on the team, defections, and so on.

I marveled at the reverence fans had for the cyclists. They'd sit outside for hours waiting for the peloton to speed by in a matter of seconds. Terry had been there for the excitement in 1971, when he spent the summer in Grenoble, France (once he learned about the wines and restaurants, he gave up on learning French.) The cyclists rode to the finish line speeding through a forest of outstretched arms and fingers, with flags and banners inches away from their faces.

Terry was overjoyed when he learned that the Tour would not be canceled, only postponed. He bloomed a little, like spring.

He wore his mask as little as possible. He customarily didn't like doing what everyone else was doing, and the material caught on his beard and pulled the mask off his nose, so he had to keep hitching it up. He restlessly drove somewhere almost every day even if it was just for a lottery ticket or a bottle of milk.

The stores didn't offer fine cheeses or ethnic delicacies, and we'd tired of the menu at the one restaurant that might match up to any one of a dozen restaurants within walking distance in Hoboken, so we rarely ordered out. Instead of being inspired by cooking at home, he succumbed to boredom and when it was his turn to cook, he churned out a few favored dishes: pasta with pesto, steak, boiled potatoes and salad, fish with a squeeze of lemon, rice, and salad. I missed being able to pop out to the bakery for a chocolate croissant for breakfast and settled for oatmeal or toast.

The outdoor tennis courts opened, and I was relieved. I'd been afraid that he wouldn't have the appetite even for tennis, but he took up his heavy bag, with two rackets, several cans of balls, a water bottle, and change of shirt and socks, and went to a nearby park to hit some balls.

Though we usually played together, at least until he had found some other tennis bums to play with, this time he didn't invite me to come with him. I didn't blame him after spending weeks and weeks looking only at me. Once we were playing at Sea Ranch and a foursome of women set up on the neighboring court. They were giggling, shrieking, and gossiping over the net. I teased Terry because I could see how annoyed he was. Occasionally, he'd find a skilled woman to play with, but he enjoyed the sweaty camaraderie of men most of the time.

"How did it go?" I asked when he got back.

"You can probably guess. When you haven't played for a while, you're pretty awful."

"So what did you do?"

"Just hit the balls across the net, practiced my serve."

"You hit them, then went and picked them up and hit them back?"

"What else is there to do? They don't have a ball machine." Sea Ranch had a ball machine.

He wasn't as relieved or enthused as I had expected. "Was anybody else there?"

"There was an old guy. We might hit around some balls."

"Was he any good?"

"I'd run rings around him." This comment was uncharacteristically disdainful. He rarely disdained individuals. Instead of picking him up, this first foray onto the courts brought him down.

The next day he woke earlier than usual, though not as early as I. I was in my office, and he sailed through the hall and out the door with his tennis bag, yelling back over his shoulder, "Going to play some tennis."

He was gone for six hours, and when he came back, I was on the phone with my son for a lengthy conversation—the pandemic was walloping him as well. It was Terry's turn to cook, and when our conversation lasted well into the time when we would be having dinner, he brought me a plate of farfalle with pesto sauce—another sweet gesture of the sort that always warmed my heart. I thought that other men would stomp around, impatient that my son was usurping their dinnertime, but Terry never behaved that way.

I didn't ask him what he had been doing when he was out of the house. Surely, he hadn't been on the tennis court for six hours.

After my conversation with my son finished, I was tired and ready for some diverting television. Terry put on a show he'd been looking forward to, a documentary about his favorite athlete of all time, even more than Roger Federer—Lance Armstrong.

And that night, he killed himself.

Chapter 41
Shock and Confusion

The EMTs, police sentinels, chaplain, social worker, coroner, detective, and what had been Terry left, and I called my children. My daughter was in Buenos Aires. She wanted to come immediately, but Argentina had shut down their airports. My son said he'd leave for Vermont the next day. He promised to be careful to wear a mask in the airport and on the plane.

I don't remember what I did that day, but it wasn't much. I was afraid I wouldn't be able to sleep that night, but I did.

If I had paid more attention to him instead of going to bed early, would it still have happened? Had I done anything to enable it? Why was he so desperate? Had something happened on the tennis court?

He left no note, not the merest hint as to why, why now.

The coroner said she was a little puzzled because there was no sign of a ligature around his neck. No red line, no bruise. Did this mean that she wondered if he had not intended to kill himself? She was too busy to explain further; their office was run ragged due to the pandemic.

I'd already determined that the torn off piece of the plastic bag lying on his neck indicated that he was pulling downward, to be sure that the bag stayed in place and he died, not that he was having second thoughts.

I wondered if the cause was some undeclared health problem. Among his papers, I found results of tests run when he saw Dr. DeMarco in January. There were several HIGHS, especially in the hematology section. Did he have incipient leukemia? I wrote a letter to the now-retired Dr. Dr. Marco, who called me back immediately. He and Terry had formed a professional friendship over their forty years together, and he was upset.

"No," he said, "there was nothing seriously wrong with him."

"What about the abnormal readings on his tests."

"Nothing to worry about. If he developed symptoms, I would have had the tests run again, but those results didn't worry me."

I asked him how his retirement was going. No, he hadn't been called back to the hospital, and yes, he was massively disappointed that he wouldn't be able to travel now. He and his wife had been dreaming of that freedom and pleasure for decades.

Twice over the past few months, Terry had briefly lost consciousness. The first time he was in the kitchen at midnight getting a glass of milk and woke up on the floor. He only told me about it when I noticed a mean bruise on his hip the next day.

"I fainted," he said. "It must have been only a few seconds. I woke up and the milk was leaking onto the floor but there wasn't much of it. It could only have lasted a second or two." He diagnosed it as an anomaly with the vagus nerve.

Two days later, he'd bent down to reach for something under the couch and suddenly careened to the floor. I was alarmed by the blank look in his eyes. He insisted he had lost his balance, but I insisted that he go to the only other doctor besides Dr. DeMarco that he was comfortable with, his cardiologist.

In those six hours he said he'd been playing tennis, had he lost consciousness again? Maybe they'd come with an ambulance and taken him to the emergency room, and he hadn't told me about it.

Maybe he discovered that he didn't have the strength in his legs for tennis anymore, or he got dizzy. He could have taken a physically alarming fall or had a fainting spell, paired it with his perceived mental deceleration, and thought he wanted to end his life before he became dependent upon me for care as a senile old man. That was possible, I supposed. Maybe he didn't want to grow old. Did people kill themselves over that?

The next morning, I went into his office. He was in charge of our finances, and I needed to see if he had given up living long ago and had not paid our bills. There were no late notices in the pile of papers on his desk. It looked utterly normal.

A half smoked joint lay an innocent witness to his death. Next to it was a matchbox from The Brass Rail, the Hoboken restaurant that our friends Michael and Marybeth used to own, a plastic bag with weed in it, and a round paper container of marijuana buds. Maybe that beatific smile when he said good-night was because he was high rather than relieved that his pain, his life, would soon be over.

I imagined he'd smoked the joint, or half of it, gotten into the chair and put the bag over his head. He was wearing a tee shirt and women's underpants. The panties were identical to mine, except larger, of course, and in slightly different colors. I had sorted them many times when I did the wash. This compromise with his cross-dressing was so familiar to me that I didn't give it a thought. But I wondered how it looked to the EMTs.

One sentence from our last, brief conversation niggled at me, though I don't recall the context. Terry was standing with his hand on the doorknob after giving me that meteor of a smile and said, "I always wondered what it would be like to be a woman."

This was not news to me but was delivered in the same mild manner with which he had spoken of suicide or cross-dressing. Just a thought, a train of thought, a temptation that bothered him now and then, something to be dealt with, managed, respected, tossed off, a remark in the middle of a harmless conversation.

Chapter 42
Doing the Necessary

I called Terry's best friends, Ralph and Peter G., to tell them Terry had died of suicide.

Ralph said, "What'd he do that for? He had everything to live for. What'd he do that for?"

Ralph said he'd thought of suicide once but had not done it, out of consideration for the people who loved him, inferring that Terry had been weak or inconsiderate. I was hurt by the implication that Terry had not loved me as much as Ralph loved his "loved ones," and I didn't want to talk to him again. But he sent me some of his flower photographs to lift my spirits. He and Terry had shared forty years of friendship, and I appreciated his efforts to comfort his friend's widow. They didn't last long, but at the time they were comforting.

Peter, who had shared over fifty years of friendship with Terry, was angry with him.

"Why?" I asked.

"Because of the mess he left."

Other than taking over the finances, which would have been a hassle even if he had died of an accident or a heart attack, there didn't appear to be any mess. Perhaps there was some nascent anger in me, but I didn't want to encourage it, didn't want to defend Terry to Peter, and didn't want the demand on my own emotional stamina that would be required to soothe him. The three of us, I, Peter, and Ralph, would have to work out our reactions alone.

The box of women's clothes in the basement was my biggest challenge over the next few weeks. I didn't know whether his cross-dressing proclivities had anything to do with his death, but they had been a constant irritant in our relationship. Throwing them away would be discarding a part of him that only he and I knew about. Now only I knew about. I would be discarding an orphaned part of him.

I didn't want the clothes in the basement when I died. What would my children think when they found them? His memory would be sullied if they found these clothes with nobody around to explain them. I didn't wear clothes like that, and the shoes were size 14. They would know they were Terry's.

I needed to talk to someone, but knew nobody in Vermont except Peter, and I couldn't ask him; he probably didn't know anything about the cross-dressing.

I phoned Joan Price. Conversations with her were always stimulating and informative. I'd been in touch with her recently because her house sits on the edge of the fire zones in California, and I worried about her.

She listened carefully as I explained my dilemma and said, "Why don't you label them for Good Will? They'll throw them away without even looking at them."

What a good idea! I went downstairs, took the clothes out, and put them in large plastic bags labeled Good Will. They sat there, monuments to the way I felt I had failed Terry. They were my mandate to understand, to reflect, to examine myself.

My son stayed with me for two weeks, then went back to San Francisco. He said, "I'm amazed at how you're taking this. I expected you'd be falling apart."

"This isn't my first rodeo, you know. It's not even the worst moment in my life. I've gotten kind of defiant. It's gotten harder to break me. Besides, my meditation has made me more even-keeled. It's a helpful tool in a situation like this."

I started my days with 7:00 meditation and allowed the tear baths when they came, but so many people I knew had been knocked down for years after a blow like this that I wasn't confident that I'd come through so smoothly. I was confused, baffled, and curious. Who was Terry? Really.

I phoned my no-nonsense friend Rita Kaehler. I hesitated to call her because I would be asking to tap her professional expertise, but I called anyway.

We caught up on her recent life, then she asked. "Tell me how you are." It was a command.

I told her that Terry had died of suicide and began to explain my confusion. "During the pandemic, it was difficult, especially for him because he was without his sports, and the move was disorienting, but our life together was so pleasant, so comfortable, that it's hard to imagine what drove him to this."

Rita was brusque, compassionate, and direct.

"We'll stipulate before we begin that nobody, nobody, nobody commits suicide unless living is more painful than dying."

"That's what I've been thinking. I don't think he would have left me unless he was suffering greatly. I'm just not sure what form that suffering took."

I told her about the cross dressing, the decision I had to make about the clothes in the basement, how he'd said he wanted to be a woman. "It sounded to me like what I mean when I say, 'I wish I were French,' you know, a fantasy."

Rita paused. "Just imagine the effort it took for him to live."

"I realize he was suffering, but what about me? I didn't marry a woman. That wasn't the deal. He didn't tell me until after we were married, and I don't know what I would have done if he had told me before. I probably wouldn't have married him. Not probably. I wouldn't have."

She laughed. "He told you after you were married? Oh my god! Ann, any other woman would have gotten outta town."

I smiled a rueful smile. "I loved him. I didn't understand how deep this went."

I told her about Mistress Fong and Terry's obsession with his weight.

Rita snipped dismissively. "This is not about his weight."

"It's an avatar for whatever else was bothering him."

"Right."

"I tried to help him lose weight, told him that I loved him no matter how heavy he was."

"But that was all beside the point," Rita said.

"You can see how it's all connected, though. It's not entirely beside the point." I blew some air out through my nose. "It's a big tangle that started the day his mother put a dress on him for Halloween when he was a boy. The whole mess is about religion and his mother and when he grew up and the dress and genetics and maybe even some of it was about him being adopted."

"He was adopted?"

"His mother was, or was not, married when he was born and his natural father signed away his parental rights and disappeared. She married John Stoeckert and John adopted Terry when he was eleven. He just said one day, 'Let's make it official,' and Terry didn't even know what he was talking about."

"What did Terry think about that?"

"He said he took it in stride, but I can't help thinking it was a big shock. He had no idea John Stoeckert wasn't his father. He was grateful to his parents, though. Didn't want to hurt them by being ungrateful."

"Interesting. Maybe the adoption's also beside the point."

"I think that if he'd made a last-ditch attempt to save his life and told me that he wanted to be a woman, other than just dressing like one, I would have stayed with him, though 76 is a bit tardy to start such a venture. But I'm not positive I could have gotten used to it, and I think he realized the risk. If he didn't tell me, our marriage was in danger, and if he did tell me, it was also in danger. He tried to tell me, but I never got the point. Either that or he didn't make himself clear. In any case, I never knew how desperate he was."

"It's as if he'd built a tree house," Rita said, "and moving even the smallest twig would bring it down. Letting on that his soul was female, even in a small way, could bring everything crashing down."

"He was afraid of being discovered, probably for all his life." Thoughts were streaming at jet speed through my head. "He was masculine to look at. There was no mannerism, no movement that suggested he felt female. When we talked about having a dog, he wanted a big one. 'A real dog,' he called it, 'not one of those little poufy things.' He was a hard-drinking carnivore, a competitive, proud sportsman. He didn't even like cream sauce."

Rita laughed. "Real men don't like cream sauce." We shared a giggle. "People who have both genders inside them offer something special. They have a strong mix of male and female."

"He was outrageously compassionate, gentle, and patient. Those are not necessarily feminine qualities. Lots of men are gentle and kind. One thing though, he had no connection with little children. 'Bring them to me when they're eight and we can have a conversation,' he said."

Rita laughed. "Wanting a uterus doesn't necessarily mean you want to be pregnant."

"I think he wanted a vagina, though I couldn't cite you a time when he said that. The terms of our relationship didn't include discussing whether he wanted a vagina. He was fascinated by vaginas, though he didn't have that fierce male urge to poke into one." I paused and Rita stayed silent as I figured out what to say next. "You know what I wonder? Why did he pick me? On the gender scale, I'm heavily female. I have no penis envy at all, no desire to kiss women, no thrill when I wear clothes a man would wear. I prefer to work, to sing, to keep company with men, as a woman."

Rita tossed off her reassurance. "He picked you. He chose you. He wanted you. You. You didn't pretend to be anything but what you are, and that is who he picked as his only wife."

I sighed in relief. "I think he loved me a lot."

"Yes. This is not your fault."

"Maybe he thought that love would conquer all. You know, change him."

Rita brushed off my ruminations. "I don't know what he thought, but he was not forced into marrying you."

"Quite the opposite, I was the one who was not inclined to marry."

"He'd never been married, right?"

"He had a long relationship with a woman who became a man."

There was a silent moment, then Rita said, "Aha."

"Yeah. Aha. That was a warning I should have heeded."

"How many years were you together?"

"Fourteen."

"And during how many of those were you happy?"

"All of them."

"Then there is no 'should have'."

We were quiet for a few moments, then Rita ended our conversation. "Imagine the effort it took him just to live every day. He didn't have the energy to do this anymore."

We hung up, my tears flowing. Poor Terry.

Chapter 43
How to Go On

As they had done so many times before, the teachings of Pema Chödrön and Thich Nhat Hanh guided and comforted me as I reeled in loss. Both had suffered massive losses and disappointments in their lives—Thich Nhat Hanh had been in Vietnam during the French and American wars there and he saw terrible things.

He taught that when in despair, I could walk slowly and observe. He promised I would find miracles in every step: birds, flowers, the sky. One day I stood in my yard and looked at my house…amazing how it gave me comfort, how the mice would always try to find a way to get in, how it sheltered family and memory. I could train my mind to find this appreciation of life's miracles: my eyes and ears, my children, the weather. My marriage to Terry had been a miracle of sorts; neither of us had expected to find such a true and devoted love so late in our lives. We each felt a sense of accomplishment that we had allowed this achievement to flourish without ruining it with jealousy, anger, greed, or pride. Or something else.

Pema Chödrön taught me about the "hungry ghosts," those inner spirits who are ready to feast on despair, anger, and all of our lowest instincts. Their favorite hour is four o'clock am, which corresponded with my experience. She taught that generosity and awareness can lift us away from the hungry ghosts. In my meditations, I began to train my mind to erase them.

Chögyam Trungpa Rinpoche's books introduced me to the idea of a spiritual warrior, giving energy and form to my efforts.

My meditations were sometimes bathed in tears because this was a sad time and crying is what to do when you're sad. Acceptance of grief cleared my head and my heart. Whether I liked it or not, grief was a building block for my future.

There was room for gratitude; I had loved someone. Isn't that what human beings seek? "Tis better to have loved and lost than never to have loved at all."

In the logic of things, losing something I truly loved would be matched by the joy of truly loving it.

In anticipating the loss of my own life, I think how I will miss those that I love. What a silly thought. It's part of the sweet pain of being alive.

Chapter 44
The Life Behind the Ashes

Over the first few weeks of mourning, I began to put the pieces together. In one sense, I was grieving Terry's loveable but fake persona forged in the harshness of Catholicism, the ignorance of the 1950s, the intolerance of the parochial schools where he was the one who objected to the constant patter of his anti-Semitic, anti-Puerto Rican, homophobic schoolmates.

Later in life, he was lucky to establish a career in a system which appreciated his brilliance, even without a Ph.D. He would, however, have had no tenure to support him if he'd come to his classroom in a dress. It wasn't until the 1990s that he came into close contact with the transgender world through Joan/Hugo, and while he was helping her to transition, he witnessed the physical and emotional stress and the alienation and misunderstanding he would run into during a transition. That would give anyone pause.

Off and on, I felt betrayed. He'd speculated more than I did about what our lives would be like when we were in our 80s, even our 90s. While we were walking along the High Line on his birthday in October, he'd said he thought we had another ten or fifteen years together. Why had he bothered to say that? Or what had changed his mind?

No subject was too intimate or too thorny for us to address, but he didn't reveal the lethal nature of his pain—a betrayal of our treasured intimacy. The only tell was that supernova smile as he said good-night, leaving me to fall asleep peacefully while he put a plastic bag over his head.

When my brother's friend Eddie hung himself in his 30s, his wife said, "He'd been so happy! We thought he was getting better." Terry had looked extra happy, too.

And there was the time he told me that he hoped I'd die before him so he could take care of me.

He'd trained as an engineer before turning to Economics. The only thing I'd ever seen him do without careful study was fall in love with me. His manner of death inconvenienced me minimally, and I assumed that he had planned it that way. It was tidy, not unlike Carlos, who blew his brains out on the grassy expanse of his front yard. Easy to clean up, just hose it off. There was nothing to clean up after Terry's death. They packed him into a plastic bag and wheeled him into the ambulance and that was all there was to it.

He'd given me unanticipated stability and comfort and balanced that out in a single blow executed in a few minutes, maybe even a few seconds, of an ordinary day. We were even.

I took the bags of women's clothes to the dump.

Terry claimed to have had a normal childhood. He suffered under a nun teacher in third grade, but spoke highly of "the brothers," his teachers in high school and college. He had friends, played sports, read a lot of books, and was rewarded for his exceptional intelligence. Even when prompted, he revealed no crushing trauma at any point in his life, just the ordinary setbacks that everyone experiences.

The poison river that ran through Terry was not a single devastating memory, it ran ceaselessly under everything good and bad. This river was visible to me only in evanescent snapshots, at distant intervals, but there was no weight attached. His words were not tinged with pain.

I grew up in the 1950s too, and if a boy had come to school in a dress, I would have thought it bizarre beyond acceptance. In those days, women were required to wear skirts or dresses (therefore, girdles and stockings) to school and work. My mother told me that Mrs. Bubb had come to a bridge afternoon in pants! "I don't know why. We all just assumed there was something wrong with her legs," she said.

Beyond the audacious Christine Jorgensen, I had no knowledge of people who felt they were transgender; the word itself wasn't even invented until 1971. I had only the least familiarity with homosexuality; it conjured men in colorful scarves behaving flamboyantly.

I had to admit that if I had felt like a man inside, I probably would have created a shield for my real self, too. I would have found someone to have children with.

Terry had done his best. He had tried every diversion: sports, an engrossing career, a bit of cross-dressing, drugs, alcohol, and last of all, falling in love with me. He thought that would be the cure for everything. We were so optimistic at our wedding.

One of my projects, of course, was to look through his papers. I was particularly looking for information about his birth and adoption. It had seemed disingenuous of him to say that he was not jolted by the discovery that the man he had always known as his father was not his father. If he'd been a toddler, the discovery could have disappeared into the haze of babyhood, but he'd been eleven. That was the only event that I knew of that could have introduced a lifelong trauma.

What I found only confounded me more. The Certificate of Birth issued by Providence Hospital in Everett, Washington, near Seattle, had him born on October 25th, 1943 at 7:30am to Paul O. and Agnes M. McDonald. The copy of the Birth Certificate issued by the Washington State Division of Vital Statistics in 1955, when Terry was adopted by John Stoeckert, has him born at 8:03am, also on October 25th, yet Terry celebrated his birthday on October 26th. It's on his driver's license and other official documents. Both birth certificates list his name as Michael Terrance McDonald. Why the changed birth date and name? Had Agnes and John Stoeckert been trying to hide Terry from Paul O. McDonald?

Agnes was born in 1910, the same year my own mother was born, and was thirty-three years old at the time. Paul McDonald was an accountant working for Atherton Construction and was 50 years old. Was Terry his first child? Had he been married before? Did Terry have half-siblings in Washington? A Certificate of Baptism dated December 5th, 1943, a little over two months after his birth, from St. Francis Parish in Seahurst, Washington, confirms his birth at Providence Hospital and lists the parents as Paul O. McDonald and Agnes M. O'Hern, not McDonald. So were they or were they not married?

My sleuthing mind imagines that Paul and Agnes were married in a civil marriage not recognized by the church, thus creating the ambiguity that Terry reflected as to whether his parents were married at the time of his birth. Being a devout Catholic, I can imagine that Agnes wanted very much to be married when she gave birth, because, among other things, she would not want her child to be called a bastard. But the ambiguity between Terry's birth certificate and the baptismal document suggests to me that it was a shotgun marriage. Who was Terry's real biological father? Did Paul marry Agnes just so she'd have a husband when her child was born, bringing the possibility of yet another man into the picture? I thought of the play *Fanny* where César marries Fanny knowing she is already pregnant with the child of a sailor who has run off to sea.

Terry kept a box made of old cardboard with all these documents in it, but did he ever look at it? How could he have had any doubt about his mother's marriage when the birth certificates issued by the State of Washington and the hospital indicate that she was married? The certificates also indicate that Agnes was a "housewife," yet she was working for the War Department. Her work status is confirmed in a later severance statement.

Was it his mother or Terry for whom this situation was too painful to discuss?

I didn't want to court an unwelcome subject, so only asked him about his parentage a few times. In his shoes, I would have been curious to know about my father, if only for genetic and health reasons, but he claimed to have no curiosity at all. I wondered if he was the child of rape, abuse, or cruel contention. Maybe Paul wanted this child and was a decent person who conceded an interest in him to Agnes only reluctantly. Apparently, since he had avoided the issue with his mother, Terry didn't know the answers to many of these questions either. It was his lack of curiosity that bewildered me, but it was his life and not my business.

Two other documents reveal big doings in December 1945, when Terry would have just turned two years old. This was the moment when Agnes and the man Terry knew as his father, John Stoeckert, moved to New York. The documents are a Relinquishment, in which Paul O. McDonald renounces his paternal rights and consents to the adoption of Michael Terrance McDonald by "any person to be chosen by Agnes," and Agnes's final paycheck as issued by the War Department, where she had been an auditor.

When they moved to New York, they changed Terry's name to Terence Michael.

The Marriage Certificate of Agnes and John Stoeckert is not among the documents, but that would be interesting to see. I wasn't going to spend an appreciable chunk of time out of my own life to track down more answers to my questions. What difference would it make now?

The human beings who could answer my questions were long dead.

The fifty Stoeckert cousins knew John as Terry's father, with only a vague idea that some funny business had happened in Seattle, and that's apparently the impression Agnes wanted to create.

John Stoeckert took on not only Agnes, with all her complications, but her son. He made good on his promise to be a father to Terry.

The only way any of this matters now is that Terry may have sustained a painful blow when he learned of his mother's shame over his birth. It was part of the Catholic heritage that Terry fled.

Chapter 45
What Memorial?

Besides poring over Terry's effects, I had to figure out what to do with his ashes. I didn't want to leave three boxes of ashes when I died: mine, Terry's, and Sherryl's. Sherryl was Terry's old friend, but my children had never heard of her, and I'd barely known her myself. Spreading her ashes along with Terry's would have been confusing and odd.

The unopened postal package containing Sherryl's ashes had been sitting in a bookcase in Hoboken and now was sitting in the same bookcase in Vermont thirteen years later. She'd entrusted Terry to sprinkle them over a body of water near New York City, but he hadn't done that. I lifted the box covered with red, white, and blue postage stamps, surprised at how heavy it was. We humans are made of minerals, I thought. Heavy metals.

My Christian Science upbringing contained no rituals surrounding death. Christian Scientists strive for freedom from the belief of death. "If a man keep my saying, he shall never see death," said Jesus. So if you see, or seem to see, death, you are not following Jesus's teachings. Something like that. It never made any sense to me so I can't explain it.

When my Christian Scientist grandmother died, my aunt Jean said, "They took her away in a station wagon," and there was no further ceremony. No ceremony for my father, only an ordinary afternoon together as a family with Bach's Double Violin Concerto in the background. That evening we met at the dinner table and my mother said, "You now sit at the head of the table," to my brother John. He stood with his hands on the back of his usual chair for a moment, then moved to the captain's chair that my father had always sat in, and that was that. I had no idea where my uncle Guy was buried, if at all, or my grandfather, my father's mother, or any of my Christian Scientist relatives. There were no places of remembrance.

I broke the mold and arranged a memorial service for my mother. She had spent her adult life doing civic work for the town of Montclair and it seemed right to gather the people she had worked with, as much to further her work as for her as a person. I don't know what became of her ashes, and nobody ever asked me. When my aunt Jean died, I buried her ashes in a park and arranged another memorial service.

Terry had given no instructions.

"You live and then you die. After that, you go back to the earth."

"Nothing happens?"

"Nothing. You're done."

The easiest thing would have been to bury the ashes of both Sherryl and Terry in the back yard of the new house in Vermont, but how would I manage the poetry of that? In the big picture, it didn't matter, but it hurt me to think of another woman, especially one who was never more than an intellectual friend, being buried next to my husband. Archaeologists finding them would deem them a couple.

We'd first seen the house in November, and through the winter I wondered what flowers and shrubs would bloom in spring. Early on, there had been a carpet of bluettes, and now there was a mass of white daisies. The apple tree was looking lively but had not produced any blossoms. Rhododendrons at the other end of the yard had some dull blooms. The lilacs in that same shady area struggled to produce a bit of color. The three stone-bordered mini-gardens needed weeding, and the soil needed replenishing, but I hadn't gotten around to serious gardening. That would be a project for later.

The property line was marked by an old stone wall. In the next yard, the stones were rubble, but someone had stacked and mortared together the stones in my yard. The two apple trees and three mini gardens filled a fifteen-foot terrace of meadow down to a lower stone wall.

The rest was a grassy yard. The terrace would be the place to bury them.

I brushed debris off the largest rock and saw engraved, "OUR BELOVED PET." I laughed out loud. When we moved in there was a dog bed in the living room, leashes, even a sack of dog food. Well, hello. Here you are, beloved pet. The place is already a graveyard.

I could bury Terry's ashes under a separate rock (this being Vermont, there were many at hand) engraved, "MY BELOVED HUSBAND," and maybe

Sherryl could go in a little corner, under a smaller rock, saying, "...and SHERRYL FEINSTEIN."

But if I sold the house, I wouldn't have a place to visit where I could revisit my love for Terry. His ashes should be in a place reserved for his memory. That shouldn't be a place I would look at every day, but someplace special.

I was nervous about spreading ashes because my father said that when his brother David spread the ashes of his wife, her teeth came flying out. I mentioned this to the man at the funeral home and he said, "You don't have to worry about that. We've changed our technology, and you can bet I sifted him real good."

A celebrant friend told me that one family hiked to the top of a steep cliff to spread the mother's ashes. They took clutches of ashes out of the container with their bare hands and threw them in the air. The ashes blew back into their faces and their hands were covered in ash. I didn't want Terry's ashes on my face.

Terry died at the end of May, and over the summer I was mired in paperwork, financial dealings, and lots of meditation, long walks, and Zoom comfort calls. In the fall, my son came to stay with me, and I turned my attention to the ashes again. If a mishap occurred like chips of Terry's teeth appearing or ashes in my face, he'd be there to help fix it. It was getting cold, and I wanted to hold our remembrance before the ground froze.

Peter and I reconnoitered and chose a spot in Aitken State Park, only ten minutes from my house. Then I began checking with the people who might attend so we could set the date.

My daughter in Buenos Aires would attend by Zoom, and of course my son would be there, and Peter. Both my brother Norris and his wife and my brother John's widow and their son lived an hour away. There would be eight of us.

And what about Sherryl? I didn't know how to contact her relatives; she had died so long ago the trail was stone cold. I ran a box opener around the top of the box holding the container of her ashes, then broke the seal of the container itself and peeked inside to see what I was dealing with. A transparent plastic bag was filled with a fine mixture in tones of gritty dull gray. I closed the top and drove to the abandoned lumbering space at the top of the hill where Terry, Peter and I had once walked. I stepped around the gate and went along the dirt path far enough so as not to be seen from the road, though passing cars were rare. I felt I was trespassing, though the logs resting on the ground had begun to decompose, suggesting that no lumbering work had been done for many years.

I took the top off the container, and said, "Godspeed, Sherryl. You were a wonderful friend to Terry." I poured out the ashes at a slow and steady pace, careful not to go so fast that they would blow into the air. This left a bright whitish mound that would be obvious to anyone walking there, so I hid the mound with a layer of autumn leaves. Sherryl had envisioned herself feeding the fishes in the waters around New York, but she would feed the trees of Vermont instead.

On the appointed day, eight of us gathered (with my daughter on Zoom) and walked to the edge of a steep ravine with a noisy stream at the bottom. There were poems, sayings, reflections, and then Peter took ashes barehanded and stood for a few moments with his eyes closed before letting go of them. My nephew squatted at the edge of the cliff for a few minutes, then threw his share of the ashes out in front of him. Nobody else cared to grab a handful and I didn't want to put my hand in the container.

I went to the edge of the ravine and bent down to tip the ashes into the void.

"Be careful," Peter said. From a video I saw later, I know that he sprinted to grab my sweater, so his best friend's widow didn't pitch down the hill.

My sister-in-law said, "What a beautiful place for him to be. The sound of the stream is so soothing."

I joined in feeling poetic. "With the first snow, these ashes will be buried, and taken gradually down the hill."

"They might end up in the ocean," Peter said.

"Or in somebody's soup," I said. They laughed, but I wasn't trying to be funny. It was true. This is how life goes on. Practically. Physically. We become part of other living beings and they become part of us.

I took the cellphone from my son to commune with my daughter as we walked back to the car. We talked about how Terry will live in our memories, in our behavior, in our appreciation of life.

Chapter 46
Epilogue

While Terry was sliding down the hill into the rushing stream, I had patched my story together without being able to swear it was all true. He'd built up an elaborate and convincing façade, but inside, he felt like a woman. In the pressures of the pandemic, where all diversions were removed and people were home alone, face to face with themselves, the pain and terror of being discovered had burst through. Without the pandemic, maybe he would have lived. Maybe not.

I realized that the husband I had loved so much was an artifact, a created persona. He was real but not real. What I was grieving was not who he really was. I loved them both, and still wonder if I could have come to accept this big man with size 14 shoes as a woman. He'd shied from making an ultimatum, "Accept me as I want to be, or else," so I didn't learn how critical the situation was, and thus could not help him.

His secret killed him. I hate that secret and am not keeping it.

He came to me in a dream. A vertical clam shell opened shedding a brilliant light, and out stepped Terry dressed in a flowing white robe, smooth cheeks, and long white hair. He was smiling and benevolent. He was a woman, and I loved him.

He came to me in another dream. I was sitting in a car with another woman. We were both separating from our husbands. When I got home in the dream, I told Terry I'd changed my mind and please to stay with me, and he said, "It's not that I don't want to live with you—I don't want to live at all."

Praise for *Daring to Date Again* – the prequel to *The Sweet Pain of Being Alive*

Praise for Ann Anderson Evans's award-winning *Daring to Date Again,* the award-winning prequel to *The Sweet Pain of Being Alive*

"…funny and introspective, filled with compassion, and written without an ounce of affectation or disingenuousness…. Her explorations are illuminating. They're also a kick, with a surprisingly uplifting effect. A candid, breezy memoir that may inspire even the most dating-averse."

—*Kirkus Reviews*

"A wise, witty memoir about a woman of a certain age who boldly and unapologetically seeks—and finds sexual adventure, and surprises herself by discovering love in the process."

—Christina Baker Kline,
author of *Orphan Train*

"Ann Anderson Evans details how a sophisticated lady of the Internet era opens doors to serious relationships [This is] a manual for sexy, smart people of a certain age, of either sex."

—Ford Burkhart, Pulitzer Prize Winner,
former editor at *The New York Times*

"*Daring to Date Again: A Memoir* is a sassy internet dating memoir with an attitude. One doesn't expect wit along with wisdom, but it's there. What's also unexpected is the spirit of adventure in a sixty-something who is willing to travel halfway across the world to Zimbabwe to meet an internet contact—but it's there, too. Most surprising of all is the quest for sexuality in older years: something few dating books even discuss. The result is best viewed as a rollicking train ride that leads to a few wrecks, excitement, and a lot of fun."

—*Midwest Book Review*

"Women of any age will find inspiration in Ann Anderson Evans' compelling tale of romantic adventure and self-reinvention. Want to know how not to act old? Live as if your story can still have the happiest of endings."

—Pamela Redmond Satran,
author of *New York Times* bestseller *How Not To Act Old*

"*Daring to Date Again* is a lively, witty, achingly honest, well-crafted account of one woman's emergence from twelve years of celibacy to become a sexual enthusiast in her sixties. You'll laugh—and sometimes worry!—as Ann jumps into bed with her Mr. Right- for-the- Moment parade. She wears her heart on her sleeve—or she wears nothing at all—and we share her adventures."

—Joan Price,
author of *Naked at Our Age: Talking Out Loud about Senior Sex*